IELTS

The Complete Guide to

General Reading

Plus 5 Complete Practice Tests

with answers

Phil Biggerton

All rights reserved

Copyright © 2014 by Phil Biggerton

No part of this book may be reproduced or transmitted in any form or by any means, electronic or mechanical, including photocopying, recording or by any information storage and retrieval system, without the written permission of the publisher, except where permitted by law.

For further information e-mail the author at:

godivabooks@gmail.com or visit: http://godivabooks.com/

ISBN: 978-0-9566332-2-4

Published by Godiva Books

Printed in the United Kingdom

The Author

Phil Biggerton has been teaching English in Asia since 1992. He became an IELTS examiner for the British Council in Taiwan and has spent over fifteen years developing his skills as an IELTS teacher. He established Godiva Books Publishing Company in 2010 and since then has published both fiction and non-fiction books for other authors as well as his own IELTS textbooks. He recently published the co-authored series **Shortcut to IELTS** with John Ross and Gary O'Connor.

CONTENTS

		Page Numbers
Getting Started	The purpose of this book / Active - Passive reading	1 - 4
Unit One	Scanning and Skimming	5 - 12
Unit Two	Selecting the best keywords	13 - 20
Unit Three	Reading techniques / How to order your questions	21 - 28
Unit Four	**Question Types 1 - 12**	29 - 80
	1. short answers	30 - 33
	2. sentence completion	34 - 37
	3. summary completion	38 - 41
	4. multiple choice	42 - 46
	5. table completion	47 - 51
	6. labelling flow charts / processes	52 - 56
	7. matching	57 - 62
	8. paragraph selection	63
	9. True, False, Not Given	64 - 68
	10. Yes, No, Not Given	69 - 70
	11. headings	71 - 78
	12. diagrams	79 - 80
General Reading	Practice Test 1	82 - 94
General Reading	Practice Test 2	95 - 107
General Reading	Practice Test 3	108 - 118
General Reading	Practice Test 4	119 - 130
General Reading	Practice Test 5	131 - 142
Blank Answer Sheets		143 - 147
ANSWERS		149 - 152
Acknowledgments		153 - 157

Getting Started

Reading is an essential skill to learn if you want to say you are fluent in a language. Without this ability you would miss out on the chance to obtain information from a wide range of different types of material like, newspapers, magazines, journals, books, leaflets and brochures. Certainly, you would never be allowed to enter a university to study if you were unable to read academic literature.

As a student entering either an undergraduate or postgraduate course, you are expected to have reached a reasonably high level of ability in all four skills – reading, writing, listening and speaking. How high these levels need to be varies from student to student (partly because of the subject they have chosen to study) and from university to university. It might be possible, for example, to start a postgraduate course at university with an overall IELTS grade of 5.0 on the condition that a presessional course is taken first at the university.

However, due to the amount of reading required to complete your studies at university, it is far better to aim for an IELTS grade of at least 6.0 in reading before you go to study. For some students this grade or higher would be a basic requirement that has to be met before they are accepted at a university to study their chosen course.

The IELTS exam

Your reading level can be measured by taking the IELTS exam. The reading section is made up of three passages with each passage being approximately 700 to 1000 words in length. These texts are not written specifically for the exam but are taken from a wide range of sources such as newspapers, books, journals, and magazines, and can be academic or non-academic in style.

Although a wide range of topics are possible, no specialist knowledge is required. However, a fairly extensive vocabulary range is needed if the text is to be completely understood. Topics can range from subjects such as tea tree oil, herbal medicine, international airports, and beetles.

Some students find that some knowledge of the subject can encourage them to "guess" the answers rather than use the text to get the correct answer. Many of these "guesses" can be wrong because the student has not read the instructions or questions carefully enough.

The test itself consists of forty questions and a time of exactly sixty minutes to finish it. At the end of the test your answers must be on the answer sheet provided. Note that, unlike the listening test, no extra time is provided to complete the answer sheet, and so a grade of zero would be given if this is blank after the allotted time.

The approximate IELTS Band Scores for the General Reading test are as follows:

Score out of 40	Grade
0	0
1	1
2	2
9	3
15	4
23	5
30	6
34	7
37	8
40	9

No two tests can ever be exactly the same, and so adjustments are made to each band score (after pretesting) to standardize the test, and ensure that no one gets a harder test than someone else. It is possible to have half grades in all four skills. So, for instance, nineteen out of forty for reading would be grade 5.5.

Question Types

Questions come in a variety of forms (twelve different questions types will be discussed later in this book) and test various skills such as scanning, skimming, reading for detail, recognizing the writer's opinion, comparing and contrasting data from two sentences (a sentence from the text and a question statement), selecting main ideas, inferring and so on.

The Purpose of this Book

The Complete Guide to General Reading takes you step by step, from a basic understanding of the IELTS exam, to a point where you have the necessary skills and confidence to take the exam. It is the intention of this book to provide you with everything you need to know to achieve a high grade in reading. It has also been specifically designed to make your journey enjoyable and less frustrating.

Many of the sample exercises in Unit Four of this book are more difficult than you will face in the real test. However, they will teach you the skills that you need to get a good grade in the actual test. The five practice tests at the back of the book are very similar to the actual General IELTS exam.

How much studying do I need to do?

Many students like to ask the question, "When can I get a grade 6.0?" or similar questions. It really is impossible for your teacher to say unless he knows you very well. Even then the answer given would be more like a guesstimate. People learn at different speeds, and the amount of homework they are prepared to do also varies from person to person. However, an approximate guide suggested by Cambridge ESOL is shown below. Someone requiring an overall grade of 6.0, for example, should expect to study (with a teacher) for between 500 and 600 hours if starting with no knowledge of English. Somebody hoping to improve from a grade 5.0 to grade 6.0 would need about 100 hours of studying.

Hours of Studying	IELTS grade
1000 – 1200 hours	7.5+
700 – 800 hours	6.5 – 7.0
500 – 600 hours	5.0 – 5.5 – 6.0
350 – 400 hours	3.5 – 4.0 – 4.5
180 – 200 hours	3.0
90 – 100 hours	1.0 – 2.0

Source: CEF and Cambridge ESOL recommended guidelines

How should I read?

This might seem a rather obvious question, but it is, nevertheless, worth asking before you start to work through this book: "How should I read?" If you think carefully about this you will probably come to the conclusion that it depends on what you are reading and why you are reading it.

Although there are many different types of reading material, it is possible to divide them into two main groups:

1. The things you read for pleasure, like novels

2. The things you read when studying (or fact finding)

When you read for pleasure you will tend to focus more on being entertained and will enjoy the actual style of writing used, but when you read to study you do so to collect facts and figures.

With both types of reading you can be either a passive reader or an active one. Which one do you think is a better way of reading?

Two Styles of Reading

The answer for both types of reading is active. This can be more easily understood if we look at the two types of reader.

The Passive Reader

The main problem with a passive reader is that they want the writer to do all of the work. They want the writer to do the thinking, the analyzing, the development of ideas, to state what is important and what isn't, what the implications of reading this are, how to use the information in the future and so on. The result is that the passive reader often reads slowly, has trouble concentrating, and has no real understanding of the structure of the thing they are reading.

The Active Reader

The active reader, on the other hand, develops an ongoing relationship with the writer. Information is read critically and any observations made are related to information previously read, or experience and knowledge obtained. An understanding of the structure of the text (even a form or newspaper) is essential if a more active approach to reading is used. Scanning, skimming and reading for further detail are all active reading skills and would not normally be used when reading for leisure.

Remember, it is your choice. Do you want to be an active or a passive reader? If you are already an active reader then well done. Do not change your style of reading as this is the correct way to read when at university. This style is also essential when studying for, and when taking, the IELTS test. If you are a passive reader you MUST change and this book will help you to do that.

UNIT ONE

Stop Reading!!!

One of the key skills to learn as you work through this book, is how to look at a text but not read it. This might sound rather strange advice, "Don't read the reading passage." To understand this, look at the text about a shipwreck and answer the question below to see why this is a useful approach to improving your reading.

Question: *"How far off shore was the wreck that Captain Bill Nagle explored?"*

The Wreck

The decade began with serious plans to explore the German Battleship Ostfriesland, a wreck lying a long way offshore in 380ft of water. During a milestone wreck diving operation Gentile, Pete Manchee and Ken Clayton made a single Heliox dive each to the wreck using custom decompression tables designed by Dr Bill Hamilton. The way now had been set; Gentile had shown that these previously inaccessible sites were now slowly becoming a possibility. In 1991 the late Captain Bill Nagle and John Chatterton led a team of experienced amateur shipwreck divers on an expedition to explore an unknown wreck at a site approximately 60 miles east of Point Pleasant, New Jersey. Upon descending to the wreck, the divers discovered what appeared to be the remains of a submarine in approximately 77 meters of water. The general appearance was that of a World War II era submarine wreck. On subsequent dives it was discovered that there were human remains aboard the wreck, but the identity of the mysterious "U-Who" would not be confirmed as that of U-869 until nearly six years later.

1. Did you read the whole text?

2. How long did it take to answer the question?

If you did read the whole text (and it is much smaller than texts in the real test) you would have taken longer to get the answer (sixty miles) than if you had used one very important reading skill that you need to learn – scanning.

Remember: looking is a lot quicker than reading.

What is scanning?

Scanning can be seen as the ability to look for individual words or short phrases of two to three words. This is done by looking for a few words rather than reading the whole text. A student who is a skilful scanner will be able to answer certain questions in the test without developing an understanding of the structure or even content of the passage. Developing this skill will save you time.

The ability to get the answer quickly from the short text about "The Wreck", was not based on understanding the whole text. Rather, it was based on reading the question carefully and realizing that the answer can be easily found by picking the words, Captain Bill Nagle (these are known as keywords) and then looking for them. Scanning the text for capital letters – C, B, N – allows you to focus on looking for (not reading) a name. Knowing that the answer is probably a number also lets you focus on looking for this as well.

Other keywords could have been picked – **shore** and **explore** – but the word, **wreck**, would have been a bad choice because it is the title (and topic) of the text. The word, **wreck**, appears seven times, and **shipwreck** once, in this paragraph. Can you think of other types of information that can be found by scanning?

In fact, any word can be found by scanning, but the easiest words to find are those with:

1. Capital letters: names of people, places, cities, countries, companies.
2. Numbers such as 1996, 21st January, 800kg, and 5 million. Remember that numbers can also be written as words like the twentieth century, eighteen fifty five, three people and so on.

Depending on the type of word you are looking for, it might be useful to have a better idea of the structure of the text. In other words, where is the answer more likely to be, at the beginning, the middle or end of the passage? This can be done by skimming.

What is skimming?

Skimming allows you to get the gist (or general understanding) of the structure of the text and what information it contains. When faced with many books to read at university (or in the case of the IELTS exam, three long reading passages), this skill is invaluable. Why read something if it is not going to give you the answer you need? Why read a sentence, a paragraph or much worse a whole text, if it is not going to lead to an answer? Do not waste time by reading what is not important.

One result of the computer age, however, has been a slowing down of skimming skills on the computer when compared with skimming on paper. Research in 1991 by Paul Muter and Paula Maurutto from the Psychology Department at the University of Toronto suggests that skimming skills should be practiced using books, rather than a computer monitor, but that comprehension and the actual speed of reading are the same for books and computers.

The way we usually read

In English, as indeed in many but not all languages, you learn to read from left to right and from the top of the page to the bottom. From a very early age you have probably been conditioned to look for information in this way. So, when you are trying to look for information, many students will try to read all of the text – from left to right and top to bottom. One problem with this is that many students read very slowly and so find answers very slowly. Remember that you only have 60 minutes for the whole test. This works out, on average, at one and a half minutes per question.

As a quick little test, read all of the passage on page 8 about Colditz and time how long it takes. Read at your normal speed. If it takes you, let's say, ten minutes then you will need at least thirty minutes to read three passages. This leaves only thirty minutes to read forty questions, find forty answers and write these answers in the answer sheet. This is not enough time for most students.

Scanning Practice

To help solve this time wasting style of finding information, and to improve your scanning skills, it is important to learn to look at the text from left to right, as well as from right to left, as you work down the page. Doing this helps stop you from reading the text as most people don't read backwards! You might also be able to start scanning in a different part of the text if you have begun to get a better idea where information is.

Look at the text on page 8 again and look for the words in List One below. Take one word at a time and try to find it very quickly. **DO NOT** mark where you find the words in the text.

List One

600	Dutch	Bill	1945
Colditz Castle	Straflager	Goering	November 6th
Jack Best	31	Poles	River Mulde
Polish	RAF	60	Germany

Now use the same text and try to find all of the words from List Two. Again look for one word at a time and **DO NOT** mark where you find the words in the text.

List Two

tailoring	chapel	sport	troops
bed	two	millet	material
cliff	national	tunnels	six
one	wood	forgery	security

NOTE - some words can be found more than once in the text.

COLDITZ

Colditz achieved fame after World War Two as the prisoner of war camp that no one could escape from. Colditz was an isolated castle built on top of a cliff, overlooking the River Mulde in central Germany. To all intents it was seemingly impossible to escape from - so the Germans believed. However, this did not mean that men did not try to do so and by putting together the best escapees from POW camps, the Germans effectively made a problem for themselves.

In the early days and months of the war, Colditz was used as a transit camp for Polish troops after the surrender of Poland. On November 6th, 1940, a handful of British RAF officers arrived, quickly followed by six British Army officers. By the end of the year, the numbers had increased and included French, Dutch and Belgium POW's. Colditz was seen by the Germans as a 'super-camp' where men who could not be held by other POW camps were sent. Officially, Colditz was a Sonderlager (Special Camp) but it was also known as a Straflager (Punishment Camp).

Men of all nationalities were brought to Colditz from 1941 onwards. It housed 600 POW's – British, French, Belgium, Dutch and Poles. Each nationality tended to stick to themselves and there was little national intermingling. The French and British did set up language lessons between themselves and some sport was played within the confines of the castle. However, the one thing that united all of them was that they were at Colditz for a good reason, and it was this defiance of German authority, despite being prisoners, that did unite all the POW's at the camp. The Germans had put together in one camp many experts in forgery, lock picking, tailoring and so on - all vital for the success of escaping. With such a collection of experts, it was only a matter of time before escape attempts were made.

Hermann Goering had visited the castle and declared it to be escape proof. He was proved to be wrong. In the time Colditz was used as a POW camp, there were many escape attempts. One hundred and twenty of these men were recaptured after breaking out, but by the end of the war, 31 POW's had successfully got back home. No other POW camp in World War Two had the same rate of success.

There was little to do at Colditz and time was spent trying to escape. Probably the most famous attempt at escape was the building of a glider in an attic above the castle chapel. When the glider was built, the idea was that the glider could be catapulted from the roof to the other side of the River Mulde with two men on board. The idea came from Bill Goldfinch and Anthony Rolt. Together with Jack Best and Stooge Wardle, they set about designing and building the glider. Using hundreds of pieces of wood - especially bed slats and floor boards - the men constructed the glider which they hoped would glide the 60 metres required to take two men to the other side of the Mulde. The skin of the glider was made from prison sleeping bags and the material's pores were sealed by boiling prison issue millet and smearing it onto the material. However, their daring idea was never put to the test as the war ended before the glider had been completed.

Tunnels were also built but the thickness of the castle walls made digging tunnels very slow work. Also by 1944, the Germans had worked out many of the ways that POW's had been using to escape and these lapses in security had been plugged. Colditz Castle was liberated on April 16th, 1945.

Scanning Practice Review

You probably found that words from List One were generally easier to find than words from List Two. Therefore, it is usually better to pick keywords like those in List One when trying to find answers from a reading passage.

You might find, however, that your scanning skills are a little weak and more practice is needed even to find the List One type keywords. To help with this, look at the nutrition fact sheet below and answer the following questions.

Nutrition Facts

Serving Size 2 tortillas (51g)
Servings Per Container 6

Amount Per Serving
Calories 110   **Calories from Fat** 10

                                              % Daily Value*

Total Fat 1g	**2%**
Saturated Fat 0g	**0%**
Trans Fat 0g	**0%**
Cholesterol 0mg	**0%**
Sodium 30mg	**1%**
Total Carbohydrates 22g	**7%**
Dietary Fiber 2g	**9%**

Vitamin A 0%	**Vitamin C** 0%
Calcium 2%	**Iron** 4%

*Percent Daily Values are based on a 2,000 calorie diet. Your daily values may be higher or lower depending on your calorie needs

	Calories	2,000	2,500
Total Fat	Less than	65g	80g
Saturated Fat	Less than	20g	25g
Cholesterol	Less than	300mg	300mg
Sodium	Less than	2,400mg	2,400mg
Total Carbohydrate		300g	375g
Dietary Fiber		25g	30g

Calories per gram
   Fat 9   -   Carbohydrate 4   -   Protein 4

Nutrition Facts

Question 1.
What type of food is this information about?

Question 2.
What percentage of your daily iron do you get per serving?

Question 3.
How many calories per gram of fat would you get?

Question 4.
How much sodium should you have per day on a 2000 calorie diet?

Question 5.
How many calories would you get with two servings?

Index

Now look at the index on page 10 and write down the page number (or numbers) where information on each topic can be found.

Topics

1. Rust
2. Hair that is short and smooth
3. How to find visual keys
4. Applying logic
5. Fabriano paper
6. Basic indenting techniques
7. Reflected light
8. Shadows on water
9. Key highlights

Index

Drawing 228, 270
Fine hair 235
Human hair 82, 84
Long Straight hair 233
Ringlets 240
Smooth short hair 236
Very short hair 237
Wavy hair 241
White, drawing 229, 232, 271
Wire hair 239, 270
Highlight 123

I
Indenting
Basic technique 67
Coated-card techniques 75
Direct method 69, 71, 235, 241
Dot method 73
Graphite method
.... 74, 75, 238, 249, 257
Indirect method 72, 73
Not used in hair 270
Stylus 25
Used in 163, 271

K
Key highlight 124, 206
Keys, visual
Basics 91, 133
Extracting 101, 133, 182, 275
Finding 132
Using 133, 185
Kneadable eraser 18

L
Layering
Basics 56, 59
Shaping form
.... 87, 164, 214, 230
Shaping form 87, 164, 214, 230

Used in 61, 185, 188, 190, 264
Lead holders 14
Light absorbency 208
Light and Shade
Cast shadows 123
Catch light 124
Contact shadows 123
Core shadows 124
Hard light 128
Highlight 123
Key highlight 124
Light source 122
Reflected light 125
Secondary highlight 124
Shadows 123
Shadows on water 207
Soft light 129
Source distance 129
Twin light sources 129
Light box 146
Lignin content 29
Line drawing, techniques 32
Line
Edges 36
Weight 35
Width 34
Local shading 229
Logic, applying 95, 116

M
Managing work
.... 94, 109, 111, 232
Margin, cleaning 277
Matting work 136
Mechanical pencils 15
Metal, rusty 191
Motivation of drawing 99
Mouth, human 79

N
Negative drawing
Basics 107, 193, 213
Benefits of method 107
Cat 163, 165, 167
Grass 110, 211
Hair 84, 230, 231, 257, 270
Latch 192
Pre-planned 109, 271
Problems, skirting 109
Rope 275
Rust 191
Spontaneous 109, 112, 270, 272
Status stalks 111
Negative space
Demonstrated 92, 220
Mask, using 94
Using 146

O
Opaque projector 148
Overhead projector 147

P
Papers
Canson 28
Fabriano 29
Illustration board 29
Ivorex 28
Mellotex 28
Plate finish 28
Strathmore 28
Types 27
Vellum finish 28
Pencils
Clutch pencil 14
Grades, choosing 36
Grades, illustrated 35
Mechanical pencil 15

Scan - Scan - Scan: Practice as much as you can

It is possible to further develop your scanning skills. If you have a friend who is also studying IELTS, or simply wants to improve this skill, you can take it in turns to ask each other to find certain words from a text that you both have. For instance, you can both buy a local paper, or photocopy a text from a magazine. Start with the more obvious words with capital letters, or numbers, and then move onto other words. Try not to pick words which are in the text too many times.

Again, **DO NOT** mark where you find the words in the text. The reason for this is because, as soon as you start to put marks on the text, you are beginning to give the reading passage structure. This then starts to make it easier and easier to find other words, because you are beginning to build up a reference of what type of information is in which paragraph. So, for the purposes of practicing this particular skill, it is better not to mark the paper. It makes you focus more on the text and not rely on what you have already found.

Both scanning and skimming require faster eye movement and the ability to process information quickly. If you find yourself moving your lips as you look for information then you are probably reading. Stop it! Also, during the times when it is essential to read in more detail, stop yourself from reading quietly to yourself. You can read more quickly mentally than you can physically say the words. Stop those lips from moving!

Skimming Practice

There are a number of different ways to skim successfully. You can develop a better understanding of structure in a text by reading the title and subtitle at the beginning of the text, sub headings (if there are any) for each paragraph or section of the text, and by looking at any illustrations or diagrams. Reading the first sentence in each paragraph can also result in a better understanding of content and structure but does take longer, possibly too long if you read quite slowly. However, all of these skills will improve with practice.

Time spent skimming books, newspapers, forms, magazines, and journals, in fact time spent skimming as many different things as you can, develops this skill.

Good writing happens because the writer understands how a reader organises information in his/her mind. In turn a good reader comes from understanding how people write. The two skills are very intimately connected and so by improving your reading skills you will be improving your writing skills and vice versa.

Combining Scanning and Skimming Skills

Look at the paragraph below and do three things,

1. Scan the text and **underline** all proper nouns (those with capital letters) and numbers.
2. Read the first and last sentence of the paragraph. **NOW - CLOSE YOUR BOOK.**
3. Write one or two sentences explaining what the paragraph is about.

The Tea Trade

When America eventually won its independence from British rule in 1783, it began its own free and independent tea trade with China. The success of this trade made some people in Britain question the wisdom of the East India Company's ongoing monopoly on British trade with the East. In 1813, the Company lost its monopoly on trade with India, but still had a complete monopoly on trade with China, which meant it was heavily dependent on the tea trade. The Company's charter was due for renewal in 1834, and in the decades before that there was a growing call for the abolition of the monopoly and the instigation of free trade with China as well. Supporters of free trade argued strongly that the Company kept tea prices artificially high in order to maximise its profits, using tactics which included restricting the supply of tea. One anonymous pamphleteer, writing in 1824, stated that 'the lordly grocers of Leadenhall Street [where the Company was based] have most scandalously abused the monopoly of which they are now in possession.' Comparing the prices of tea sold at auction in London with the prices at auction in Hamburg and New York, he thundered that 'the monopoly of the tea trade enjoyed by the East India Company costs the people of this country, on average, not less than two million, two hundred thousand pounds sterling a year!'

Even if you do not know exactly what the paragraph is about, spending a little time on scanning and skimming will have given you some useful information. Also, by underlining certain words and numbers you have also added structure to the text.

Remember that the more you know about the structure of each passage you read, the more chance there is that you will know where to look for answers. This will save you a lot of valuable time, time that you can spend more effectively on detailed reading of the sentences where you know answers are likely to be.

A possible summary on the tea trade text could be:

This paragraph is about the tea trade in the late 18th and early 19th century and the rivalry between America and Britain. The East India Company created a tea monopoly which resulted in very high prices in London.

UNIT TWO

Keywords

As we saw in Unit One, the ability to find individual words or short phrases through scanning is an important skill to develop. This will enable you to find answers to questions much more quickly because of this, particularly when using proper nouns (capital letters) and numbers. Not all paragraphs (or texts) have as many proper nouns or numbers as the examples shown in Unit One but this is one reason why some reading passages might be harder than others.

Any word that you choose from a question sentence to help you find the answer can be called a keyword. The selection of good keywords is an essential part of finding answers to questions more quickly and more accurately. This unit, therefore, will explore in a little more detail how to select good keywords.

Instructions: Look at the questions below that go with the text on pages 14 and 15 and underline what you think is the best keyword for each question. Then write down what type of answer you expect to find.

DO NOT turn the page. Only look at the question sentences on this page when you are selecting the keywords

Questions 1 - 8

Answer the questions below.

*Choose **NO MORE THAN THREE WORDS AND/OR A NUMBER** from the passage for each answer.*

	Question	What answer do you expect?
1	How old is the Armenian shoe?	_____
2	What was found in the shoe?	_____
3	What environmental factors protected the shoe?	_____
4	What was the shoe covered with?	_____
5	How old was the shoe originally thought to be?	_____
6	What two things were tested to determine the age of the shoe?	_____
7	Who found the shoe?	_____
8	When did Irish people wear similar shoes?	_____

Now find the answers from the reading passage on pages 14 and 15. There are eight questions and so it should (on average) take twelve minutes to complete. Don't forget to quickly scan the text first for proper nouns and numbers and underline what you find.

World's oldest leather shoe found in Armenia

A perfectly preserved shoe, 1,000 years older than the Great Pyramid of Giza in Egypt and 400 years older than Stonehenge in the UK, has been found in a cave in Armenia. The 5,500 year old shoe, the oldest leather shoe in the world, was discovered by a team of international archaeologists.

The cow-hide shoe dates back to 3,500 BC (the Chalcolithic period) and is in perfect condition. It was made of a single piece of leather and was shaped to fit the wearer's foot. It contained grass; although the archaeologists were uncertain as to whether this was to keep the foot warm or to maintain the shape of the shoe, a precursor to the modern shoe-tree perhaps? "It is not known whether the shoe belonged to a man or woman," said lead author of the research, Dr Ron Pinhasi, University College Cork, Ireland "as, while small, (European size 37; US size 7 women), the shoe could well have fitted a man from that era." The cave is situated in the Vayotz Dzor province of Armenia, on the Armenian, Iranian, Nakhichevanian and Turkish borders, and was known to regional archaeologists due to its visibility from the highway below.

The stable, cool and dry conditions in the cave resulted in exceptional preservation of the various objects that were found, which included large containers, many of which held well-preserved wheat and barley, apricots and other edible plants. The preservation was also helped by the fact that the floor of the cave was covered by a thick layer of sheep dung which acted as a solid seal over the objects, preserving them beautifully over the millennia!

"We thought initially that the shoe and other objects were about 600-700 years old because they were in such good condition," said Dr Pinhasi. "It was only when the material was dated by the two radiocarbon laboratories in Oxford, UK, and in California, US that we realised that the shoe was older by a few hundred years than the shoes worn by Ötzi, the Iceman."

Three samples were taken in order to determine the absolute age of the shoe and all three tests produced the same results. The archaeologists cut two small strips of leather off the shoe and sent one strip to the Oxford Radiocarbon Accelerator Unit at the University of Oxford and another to the University of California – Irvine Accelerator Mass Spectrometry Facility. A piece of grass from the shoe was also sent to Oxford to be dated and both shoe and grass were shown to be the same age.

The shoe was discovered by Armenian PhD student, Ms Diana Zardaryan, of the Institute of Archaeology, Armenia, in a pit that also included a broken pot and wild goat horns. "I was amazed to find that even the shoe-laces were preserved," she recalled. "We couldn't believe the discovery," said Dr Gregory Areshian, Cotsen Institute of Archaeology at UCLA, US, co-director who was at the site with Mr. Boris Gasparyan, co-director, Institute of Archaeology, Armenia when the shoe was found. "The crusts had sealed the artefacts and archaeological deposits and artefacts remained fresh dried, just like they were put in a can," he said.

The oldest known footwear in the world, to the present time, are sandals made of plant material, that were found in a cave in the Arnold Research Cave in Missouri in the US. Other contemporaneous sandals were found in the Cave of the Warrior, Judean Desert, Israel, but these were not directly dated, so that their age is based on various other associated artefacts found in the cave.

Interestingly, the shoe is very similar to the 'pampooties' worn on the Aran Islands (in the West of Ireland) up to the 1950s. "In fact, enormous similarities exist between the manufacturing technique and style of this shoe and those found across Europe at later periods, suggesting that this type of shoe was worn for thousands of years across a large and environmentally diverse region," said Dr Pinhasi.

"We do not know yet what the shoe or other objects were doing in the cave or what the purpose of the cave was," said Dr Pinhasi. "We know that there are children's graves at the back of the cave but so little is known about this period that we cannot say with any certainty why all these different objects were found together." The team will continue to excavate the many chambers of the cave.

A review of the Oldest Shoe exercise

Did you find that the keywords you chose helped you? Did you find it easier to find the questions when you knew the kind of information you were looking for? Also, if you scanned the text first for proper nouns and numbers, you could have found four of the answers before you had even read the questions. These would have been **Question 1** (5,500 years old), **Question 5** (600-700 years old), **Question 7** (Ms. Diana Zardaryan) and **Question 8** (1950s).

The selection of good keywords and scanning can be a very quick and efficient way of getting information. As soon as you know that you are looking for a name of a person, a city, a country - indeed any kind of proper noun - or a number of some kind, you can rescan the text looking at what you have underlined. No reading required. Detailed reading of only one sentence might be necessary so that you can check that the word you have found is the correct one and fits the question.

Selecting the best Keywords

As you have already seen, the best keywords to take from a question sentence are usually proper nouns and numbers. There are times, however, when both proper nouns and figures are more difficult to find. Can you think why this might happen?

Proper Nouns

The first situation to cause problems is when the proper noun is the subject of the text. For example, you might see a question in a reading passage entitled, "**Paris in the modern world**", that asks:

What are some of the major industries in Paris?

Unless you scan the text before reading the question, you do not know how many times the word Paris appears in the text. It is possible, because Paris seems to be the focus of the topic, that the word will appear many times. Imagine a situation where the text has the word **Paris** in eight different sentences. Which sentence should you read to get the answer? Do any of the sentences have the answer? Maybe you read all eight sentences and end up with no answer. Imagine how much time you have wasted. What would be a better keyword to pick from the question above?

Scanning the text might already have told you that several paragraphs focused on jobs or the economy in Paris. Words you might have underlined could have been percentages relating to the economy and names of companies relating to jobs. The best keyword to have picked from this question would have been - **industries**.

Remember:

Picking keywords from the heading (or sub-heading) are probably going to waste time.

Numbers

Like proper nouns, numbers can be seen very quickly when scanning a text. If you don't agree then this is a sign that you must keep practising the scanning exercises introduced to you in Unit One. There are some situations, however, when numbers become harder to see. The main problem is when the number has been changed from numerals like (1, 2, 3, 4, 5 and so on) to actual letters (one, two, three, four, five). It is obvious which ones are easier to see. If you don't believe this then scan the paragraph below and underline any numbers you see.

San Francisco Earthquake

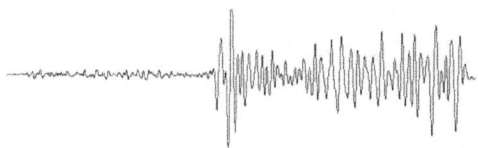

A major earthquake struck San Francisco, and the coast of northern California, on Wednesday April 18, 1906, at 5:12 A.M. This quake was estimated at a magnitude of from 7.8 to 8.3. The main shock, lasting from forty-seven seconds to almost one minute, occurred about two miles offshore from this major California city. However, shaking from this quake was felt all the way from Coos Bay, Oregon, the state directly north of California, southward to Los Angeles and San Juan Bautista in Southern California. According to the U.S. Weather Bureau on Post Street in San Francisco, the quake was felt over an area of about 375,000 square miles.

Did you find all of the numbers? There are nine of them altogether.

Little tricks that might confuse you

Another problem is when the question states something like:

> *What happened in the middle of the 20th Century to greatly influence the American civil rights movement?*

The answer you are looking for might be in a sentence stating:

> *The assassination of Martin Luther King in 1968 had a profound effect on the civil rights movement in America.*

Looking for either **20th** or **Century** would not have helped you and would have wasted time. Also, you can see that 1968 is not exactly in the middle of the 20th Century but around "the middle". This type of situation can happen in the IELTS reading test and, although there is no way of telling when this might happen, you must always be prepared. Time can be lost if you are not prepared for these little tricks that might be used to hide the answer.

It is possible that the answer to this type of question would be made easier if you scan the text before answering the question as it might show that information is in chronological (time) order.

Picking poor keywords can waste time

It is fairly obvious that picking the best keyword from every question sentence is what you have to try and do. If every question sentence had a proper noun or number to pick as a keyword, the IELTS test would suddenly have become much, much easier. However, this will never happen.

It is possible, however, that the following might happen:

1. You read a question sentence.
2. You pick a keyword.
3. You look for the keyword in the text.
4. You can't find the word you chose.
5. You read the question sentence again.
6. You pick another keyword.
7. You look for this keyword in the text and still find nothing.

More and more time is being taken in trying to answer this one question, leaving less and less time to answer enough questions to get the grade you need. And remember, there is never any guarantee that you can answer the question, even when you find the correct sentence. A lot of time gone but no answer!

To illustrate this more clearly, imagine you have picked the word, **produce**, as your keyword after reading a question sentence about salmon. You then start to scan the text for your keyword. You start with the first paragraph and progress through the whole text until you reach the end. You don't find the original keyword – **produce** – even though it is there and would have led you to the correct answer. A need for more scanning practice is called for if this happens.

Another possibility is that you don't find the keyword because you don't know the synonym that has replaced it. For instance, do you know the word, **spawn**? This is a synonym of the keyword used here.

This does not mean that verbs are bad keywords. In many cases it is possible to find the correct sentence in the text – the sentence with the answer in – by picking a verb as a keyword. However, begin to develop your confidence in picking keywords. If you think it is the best choice – pick it. But also begin to know when you have spent enough time on a question and need to move onto the next question.

Synonyms

Look at the selection of words below and decide which ones are synonyms of the keyword, **to build**.

1. compile
2. develop
3. establish
4. fabricate
5. form
6. formulate
7. improve
8. institute
9. manufacture
10. produce
11. strengthen
12. synthesize

Did you pick all of them? If you did, then you did very well. Remember, however, that not all synonyms of a particular word can be used in the same context because exact meanings can vary from word to word and context to context. For instance, you can hire or rent a car but you can only hire a person (not rent a person). These examples show the need to continue to develop your vocabulary range as much as possible through reading.

Vocabulary Level Check

Knowing how good your vocabulary range is can be tested in many different ways, but the method used here is based on a series of vocabulary based frequency lists developed by Batia Laufer & Paul Nation.

There are eighteen questions in each test and you have to decide which word is missing from each sentence. The first few letters have been given to you to help. Read each sentence carefully and try to fully understand the meaning. Then write down what you think the answer is for each sentence.

It is suggested that if you score below fifteen out of eighteen on either of the two tests given here that your vocabulary range is below university level and work needs to be done to further improve your range.

University Level Check – One

1	I've had my eyes tested and the optician says my vi............... is good.
2	The anom............... of his position is that he's chairman of the committee, but cannot vote.
3	In their geography class, the children are doing a special pro............... on North America.
4	In a free country, people are not discriminated against on the basis of colour, age, or s...............
5	A true dem............... should ensure equal rights and opportunities for all citizens.
6	The drug was introduced after medical res............... indisputably proved its effectiveness.
7	These courses should be taken in seq............... not simultaneously.
8	Despite his physical condition, his int............... was unaffected.
9	Governments often cut budgets in times of financial cri...............
10	The job sounded interesting, but when he realized what it involved, his excitement sub...............
11	Research ind............... that men find it easier to give up smoking than women.
12	In a lecture, a lecturer does most of the talking. In a seminar, students are expected to part............... in the discussion.
13	The airport is far away. To en............... that you catch your plane, you'll have to leave early.
14	It's difficult to ass............... a person's true knowledge by one or two tests.
15	The new manager's job was to res............... the company to its former profitability.
16	Although he didn't do well in the midterm exam, he got the highest mark in the fi...............
17	His plan to leave home wasn't well thought out. It was not based on rat............... considerations.
18	The challenging job required a strong, successful, and dyn............... candidate.

Final Score ___ / 18

UNIT THREE
Reading Passages 1, 2 and 3

This unit will look more closely at the general approach needed to take the IELTS reading test. Although there are many types of questions, the approach you can take in answering each question is surprisingly similar from question type to questions type.

How to order your Questions

Many of the different question types that you will learn about later in this book have their answers in order. The first answer nearer the beginning of the text and the last answer nearer the end of the text. This is an important point to realise because it leads onto other time savings skills. This knowledge gives you two possible ways of taking the reading part of the IELTS exam:

Method One: in order (from question 1 through to question 40)

Method Two: out of order - selecting the easiest questions to answer first

Try to think of the advantages and disadvantages of both approaches.

	Advantages	Disadvantage
Method One		
Method Two		

Look at an example text about the Dodo (on pages 22-23) to see how Method Two can help you more than Method One in answering the more difficult questions. Scan the text that follows, **The Dodo – Stage One**, for proper nouns and numbers. Underline them as you find them.

DO NOT try to find the answers yet!

The Dodo (Stage One)

The dodo formerly known as 'Didus ineptus' has been renamed 'Raphus cuculatus'. The dodo is the most famous extinct species in the history of planet Earth. Its first contact with Europeans was in 1598, when a Dutch expedition headed by Admiral Jacob Cornelius van Neck landed on an island, thick with dense forests of bamboo and ebony, off the east coast of Africa. The island was named Mauritius by the adventurous and artistic admiral – the first man to draw the extraordinary and unique flightless bird, now universally known as the dodo (from the Dutch word '*dodoor*' meaning sluggard). The demise of the dodo has been attributed to hungry Dutch sailors en route to the Spice Islands of Indonesia. They would take a dinner break on the tropical island and consume the defenceless dodo, but it was clearly an acquired taste as the sailors named it '*valghvogel*'- meaning disgusting bird.

The island of Mauritius is only 10 million years old and until the arrival of European settlers, there were no island predators to threaten the easy-going existence of the dodo, a bird that had evolved from the African fruit-eating pigeons of the genus 'Treron'. This benign, predator free paradise had allowed the dodo to evolve into a pedestrian bird with tiny wings unable to rise even a few inches off the ground. The dodo was no match for the cunning, domestic pets of Europe and within less than a 100 years after the first landing of van Neck and his band of adventurers, the dodo was extinct -- the last egg devoured, no doubt, by an overstuffed rat whose ancestors had emigrated from the sewers of Amsterdam with the original Dutch colonists.

The popular image of a fat and stupid creature comes from the celebrated painting of the dodo by Jan Savery (1589–1654). On his visits to the Oxford University Museum, Lewis Carroll was inspired by this image and the only remaining dodo skull and claw (both are still on display there), to create his own fictional version for 'Alice's Adventures in Wonderland' - "When they had been running half an hour or so, the dodo suddenly called out, 'The race is over', and they all crowded round it, panting, and asking, 'But who has won?'"

That image of the weird, flightless, dim-witted dodo is now being challenged by contemporary scientific research. Dr Andrew Kitchener has created two life-size reproductions of the dodo – one is housed in the Royal Museum of Scotland in Edinburgh and the other is in the Oxford University Museum. They are based on research using hundreds of actual dodo skeletons and bones unearthed by naturalists in the Mare aux Songes swamp in South-East Mauritius.

The new slimmer, streamline dodo is very different from the fat, cuddly buffoon celebrated in the picture of Jan Savery. Dr Kitchener's research presents us with a lithe, active, smart dodo superbly adapted to live and survive prosperously in the forests of its native Mauritius. The popular image of a fat, immobile, flightless dodo was drawn by Savery and his contemporaries because the live specimens that they used as models had been shipped over to Europe on a diet of ships biscuits and weevils and then overstuffed by their over-zealous owners as they exhibited them to the general public.

In 1991 further credence was given to this new image of the dodo, when a series of long-lost drawings by Harmanszoon dating from 1601 were discovered in the Hague after having been lost for over 150 years. These drawings confirm the thin streamline image first seen in van Neck's drawings of the dodo from 1598. We will never know exactly what the Dodo looked like, but this enduring symbol of casual, careless extinction will continue to fascinate generations to come.

Selecting the best questions

Now, after you have scanned the text and underlined proper nouns and numbers, look at the seven questions below. Select the best keyword from each question and decide which **THREE** questions you will do first.

DO NOT look for the answers yet.

Questions 1 - 7

Complete the sentences below.

*Choose **NO MORE THAN THREE WORDS AND/OR A NUMBER** from the passage for each answer.*

	Question	Best Keyword	Order
1	The Dutch would rest in _____ on the way to Indonesia.		
2	The dodo is a descendant of the _____ .		
3	It was impossible for the dodo to fly because it had _____.		
4	It took under _____ for the last egg to be consumed.		
5	Lewis Carroll saw parts of a dodo in a _____ .		
6	_____ discovered an abundant source of skeletons.		
7	More recent ideas of the Dodo suggest that it was _____ .		

The Dodo (Stage Two)

One possible way to do these questions

To show you the advantages of doing most of these question types out of order, lets imagine that you have decided that the best keywords for each question (and the question order for the first three questions) are:

	Best Keyword	Question Order
1.	Indonesia	1
2.	descendant	
3.	fly	
4.	egg	
5.	Lewis Carroll	2
6.	skeletons	3
7.	recent	

Remember, answers can often be found with more than one keyword. This means that not everyone will pick the same keyword but still get the correct answer. However, look at what has been picked here and see if you agree. The order of answering the questions is based on how good you think the keywords are, how easy you think the keywords are to find, and how easy you think the answers are to find. Answers for both questions 1 and 6 are likely to be proper nouns.

Questions 1, 5 and 6

Go back to pages 22 and 23 and do the first three questions in the order suggested in the table above – Questions 1, 5 and 6. **DO NOT** look for Questions 2, 3, 4 and 7. Also, time how long it takes you to find these three questions.

OK. How long did it take you to find questions 1, 5 and 6? If it took you less than three minutes, you did very well. The text is now shown again on page 26. Notice that four different types of information have been scanned and underlined and not just proper nouns and numbers.

- **Proper nouns** – e.g. Mauritius, Lewis Carroll, Europe
- **Numbers** – e.g. 1598, 150 years, 1991
- **Words in italics** – e.g. *'dodoor'*, *'valghvogel'*
- **Words or short phrases in quotation marks** – e.g. "The race is over", 'Didus ineptus'

You will notice that in the case of the examples for words in italics, they are also in quotation marks.

By scanning for these four types of information, you can already tell that the text mentions:

- **People** – e.g. Jan Savery
- **Years and periods of time** – e.g. 1601, 1589-1654
- **Buildings** – e.g. Royal Museum of Scotland
- **Countries, Cities, Places** – e.g. Oxford
- **Different names for the dodo** – e.g. 'Raphus cuculatus'

This is a huge help in deciding what information each paragraph contains. You can now see the highlighted results of the three answers for Questions 1, 5 and 6 in The Dodo (stage Two) on page 26.

You should have found that the answers were:

Question 1 - Mauritius
Question 5 - museum
Question 6 - naturalists

You need to write - Naturalists - with a capital letter in the answer sheet because it comes at the beginning of the sentence in the question.

You can now be fairly certain that:

- Questions 2, 3 and 4 are between answers 1 and 5
- Question 7 is after question 6

This means that all of the questions still to answer have become easier because their general position in the text has been located.

Remember - answers for most question types are in order.

Now try to find the four other questions – 2, 3, 4 and 7 – using the keywords that you picked from the text. Try to find all four answers in six minutes or less. Remember, on average you have one and a half minutes per question.

Now - turn to page 26 and answer questions 2, 3, 4 and 7

The Dodo (Stage Two)

The dodo formerly known as **'Didus ineptus'** has been renamed **'Raphus cuculatus'**. The dodo is the most famous extinct species in the history of planet **Earth**. Its first contact with **Europeans** was in **1598**, when a **Dutch** expedition headed by **Admiral Jacob Cornelius van Neck** landed on an island, thick with dense forests of bamboo and ebony, off the east coast of **Africa**. The island was named **Mauritius** by the adventurous and artistic admiral – the first man to draw the extraordinary and unique flightless bird, now universally known as the dodo (from the **Dutch** word **'dodoor'** meaning sluggard). The demise of the dodo has been attributed to hungry **Dutch** sailors en route to the **Spice Islands** of **Indonesia**. They would take a dinner break on the tropical island and consume the defenseless dodo, but it was clearly an acquired taste as the sailors named it **'valghvogel'** - meaning disgusting bird.

Answer to Question 1

The island of **Mauritius** is only **10 million years old** and until the arrival of **European** settlers, there were no island predators to threaten the easy-going existence of the dodo, a bird that had evolved from the **African** fruit-eating pigeons of the genus **'Treron'**. This benign, predator free paradise had allowed the dodo to evolve into a pedestrian bird with tiny wings unable to rise even a few inches off the ground. The dodo was no match for the cunning, domestic pets of **Europe** and within less than a 100 years after the first landing of van **Neck** and his band of adventurers, the dodo was extinct -- the last egg devoured, no doubt, by an overstuffed rat whose ancestors had emigrated from the sewers of **Amsterdam** with the original **Dutch** colonists.

Answers to Questions 2, 3 and 4 in this area

The popular image of a fat and stupid creature comes from the celebrated painting of the dodo by **Jan Savery (1589–1654)**. On his visits to the **Oxford University Museum**, **Lewis Carroll** was inspired by this image and the only remaining dodo skull and claw (both are still on display there), to create his own fictional version for **'Alice's Adventures in Wonderland'** - "When they had been running half an hour or so, the dodo suddenly called out, 'The race is over', and they all crowded round it, panting, and asking, 'But who has won?'"

Answer to Question 5

That image of the weird, flightless, dim-witted dodo is now being challenged by contemporary scientific research. **Dr Andrew Kitchener** has created two life-size reproductions of the dodo – one is housed in the **Royal Museum of Scotland** in **Edinburgh** and the other is in the **Oxford University Museum**. They are based on research using hundreds of actual dodo skeletons and bones unearthed by naturalists in the **Mare aux Songes** swamp in **South-East Mauritius**.

Answer to Question 6

The new slimmer, streamline dodo is very different from the fat, cuddly buffoon celebrated in the picture of **Jan Savery**. **Dr Kitchener's** research presents us with a lithe, active, smart dodo superbly adapted to live and survive prosperously in the forests of its native Mauritius. The popular image of a fat, immobile, flightless dodo was drawn by **Savery** and his contemporaries because the live specimens that they used as models had been shipped over to **Europe** on a diet of ships biscuits and weevils and then overstuffed by their over-zealous owners as they exhibited them to the general public.

In **1991** further credence was given to this new image of the dodo, when a series of long-lost drawings by **Harmanszoon** dating from **1601** were discovered in the **Hague** after having been lost for over **150 years**. These drawings confirm the thin streamline image first seen in van **Neck's** drawings of the dodo from **1598**. We will never know exactly what the dodo looked like, but this enduring symbol of casual, careless extinction will continue to fascinate generations to come.

Answer to Question 7 in this area

Review of The Dodo

Because most question types have their answers in order, you can use this "out of order" method of answering for most of the reading test. There are usually about twelve questions for each text and these could be divided into 3 or 4 different types of question. For each set of questions you need to go back to the beginning of the text and start scanning for keywords again.

Which Reading Passage is the Easiest – One, Two or Three?

Let's look at another question that seems very obvious, "Which reading passage is the easiest – One, Two or Three?" The first thought is probably to answer – "Reading passage One" – but let's think about this more carefully and think about what you have learnt so far.

When you do a practice test, or a real IELTS exam, where do you think you make the most mistakes? Reading passage One, Two or Three? Does it seem to vary from test to test? With the real exam it is impossible for you to know where you made mistakes but when you do practice tests you can see. Have a look at some of your previous tests (or wait until you have done some) and look at which passage was harder.

Answer these questions:

- Do you make most of your mistakes in reading passage Three?
- Are certain question types harder than others?

If you said, for example, "I find heading type questions very difficult" would reading passage One become harder if it contained heading questions or is reading passage Three still the hardest?

Also, do you always have more problems with vocabulary in reading passage Three or do you find that any text can be a problem because the words are more difficult to understand?

Thinking about the test in this way helps to show you that the type of topic and the type of questions in a text might make one reading passage harder than another. Remember, everyone is different. Different likes and dislikes for the question types and having different vocabulary ranges will make different students see each IELTS exam in a different way from the next student.

Ideally, you should be good at every question type but this takes time, and this is something not every student has. Students are eager to take the test and a deadline (the start of their course at university) has to be met. However, it is important for you to practice every skill shown in this book and try to become skilful in each one.

Where should you start?

By now you should be thinking that it might not be a good idea to take the IELTS exam by starting with question one and working through the whole test in order and finishing with question forty. So, how do you know which are the more difficult questions? Which order should you do the questions in?

Complete the table below that reviews what you have studied in Units One, Two and Three.

1.	What do you scan a text for?
	       a. ....
	       b. ....
	       c. ....
	       d. ....

2.	What do you skim a text for?
	       a. ....
	       b. ....
	       c. ....
	       d. ....
	       e. ....

3.	How can you decide which keywords are not so good?
	       a. ....
	       b. ....

4.	How can you decide what are good keywords?
	       a. ....
	       b. ....
	       c. ....
	       d. ....

5.	What questions do you do first?
	       a. ....
	       b. ....

UNIT FOUR
Question Types

This unit will introduce the twelve different question types commonly used in the IELTS exam. Each complete test of three reading passages will use a selection of these for the 40 questions. As you work through Unit Four, you will see that most question types rely on the skills and strategies discussed in previous units, scanning, skimming, reading for detail, the selection of good keywords, underlining these keywords, the development of a clearer understanding of the structure of the text, and an awareness of what type of answer you are looking for.

The table below lists the different question types shown in this book and if the answers are usually in order. As you can see, most of them are. Use this knowledge to your advantage when studying the different question types and when you do the five complete practice tests at the back of this book.

	Question Type	Are answers usually in order?	
1	Short answers	YES	
2	Sentence completion	YES	
3	Summary completion	YES	
4	Multiple choice	YES	
5	Table Completion	YES	
6	Labeling Flow Charts / Processes	YES	
7	Matching		NO
8	Paragraph Selection		NO
9	True, False, Not Given	YES	
10	Yes, No, Not Given	YES	
11	Headings		NO
12	Diagrams	YES	

1 - Short Answers

In this question type, you are given a number of questions that can be answered in a few words - usually between one to three - that must be taken from the text. The instructions will tell you how many words you can use for any particular set of questions.

Look at the paragraph below and try to answer the two questions that follow:

US food waste worth more than offshore drilling

Recent estimates suggest that 16 per cent of the energy consumed in the US is used to produce food. Yet at least 25 per cent of food is wasted each year. Michael Webber and Amanda Cuellar at the Center for International Energy and Environmental Policy at the University of Texas at Austin calculate that this is the equivalent of about 2,150 trillion kilojoules lost each year. That's more than could be gained from many popular strategies to improve energy efficiency. It is also more than projections for how much energy the US could produce by making ethanol biofuel from grains.

Questions 1 - 2

Answer the questions below.

*Choose **NO MORE THAN THREE WORDS AND/OR A NUMBER** from the passage for each answer.*

1   How much food does the US waste every year?
2   How much energy could be saved annually if food was not wasted?

These are quite easy questions to answer and are based on the skills taught in previous units. Poor keywords for question one would be – **US, food, waste,** – because these are in the title of the reading passage. This leaves the word, **year** as probably the best keyword to pick. This will take you to two sentences with the word, **year** in. The first of these is the correct sentence.

Question two has a choice of three potential keywords – **energy, saved, annually**. All three keywords will take you to the correct sentence but you need to think more carefully about this. The keyword, **energy** is part of the title of the centre – *"Center for International Energy and Environmental Policy"* - **saved** can help if you realise that this is the opposite of the word **lost** in the phrase – *"2,150 trillion kilojoules lost"* – and the word, **annually** has the same meaning as the phrase – *"each year"*.

Remember - each question starts with the phrase - How much.

You know, therefore, that the answer must be a quantity and so probably a number. So, when thinking of keywords also think about what kind of answer you are looking for as this can help you answer the question more quickly.

Now answer the eight questions that follow the reading passage below about the dingo.

The Dingo – An Australian Pest

The origins of the dingo are obscure and there is much controversy connected with this. It is not truly native to Australia but is thought to have arrived between 3,500 and 4,000 years ago. Whatever its origins, the dingo was a highly valued companion to the aborigines. They were hunting companions, guard dogs, and they kept them warm at night.

Some believe they were brought here on rafts or boats by the ancestral aborigines. It has also been suggested that they came with Indonesian or South-East Asian fishermen who visited the northern coast of Australia.

The dingo can be found in all areas of Australia - from harsh deserts to lush rainforests. The highly adaptable dingo is found in every habitat and every state of Australia, except Tasmania. In deserts, access to drinking water determines where the animal can live. Pure-bred dingo numbers in the wild are declining as man encroaches deeper and deeper into wilderness areas, often accompanied by his domestic dog.

The dingo is different from the modern dog in several ways: it does not bark, it has a different gait, and its ears are always erect. Dingoes are naturally lean and they are usually cream to reddish-yellow with white points, some are black with tan points. An adult dingo stands more than 60cm high and weighs about 15kg. It is slightly smaller than a German Shepherd.

In its natural state the dingo lives either alone or in a small group unlike many other wild dog species which may form packs. Dingoes have a clearly defined territory which they rarely leave and which they protect from other dingoes, but which may be shared with other dingoes when they form a group to hunt larger prey. The size of the home territory varies according to the food supply. Dingoes hunt mainly at night. Groups are controlled by a dominant male. Members of a group maintain contact by marking rocks and trees within their territory, and by howling, particularly in the breeding season.

The dingo's diet consists of native mammals, including kangaroos, although domestic animals and some farm stock are also on the menu. This makes the animal unpopular with farmers. The dingo is thought to have contributed to the mainland extinction of the thylacine (Tasmanian tiger) through increased competition for food.

The dingo is an intelligent animal. It is no more dangerous to man than any other feral dog. The natural prey of the dingo is small mammals and ground-dwelling birds, but with the introduction of white settlement, they became such a menace to sheep, calves and poultry that measures had to be taken in an attempt to control them, such as "dog-proof fences".

Dingoes start breeding when they reach the age of one or two but only the dominant members within an established group breed. They breed only once a year. Mating usually occurs in autumn/early winter and after a gestation of nine weeks (same as domestic dogs) a litter averaging 4-5 pups is born, which are reared in a hollow log, a rock-shelter, or an old rabbit warren. Both parents take part in raising the pups. The pups are fully grown at seven months of age. A dingo may live for up to ten years.

Wild dingoes are wary of humans and do not attack unless provoked. They will approach camps in the bush looking for food or perhaps out of curiosity. Dingoes can be kept as pets but should be obtained at a very young age to enable them to bond with humans. Even when raised from pups they never seem to lose their instinct for killing poultry or small animals. Not all states in Australia allow dingoes to be kept as pets and a permit is required. The export of dingoes is illegal.

Dingoes and domestic dogs interbreed freely resulting in very few pure-bred dingoes in southern or eastern Australia. This threatens the dingo's ability to survive as a separate species. Public hostility is another threat to the dingo. Because it takes some livestock, the dingo is considered by many to be a pest.

Questions 1 - 8

Answer the questions below.

*Choose **NO MORE THAN THREE WORDS AND/OR A NUMBER** from the passage for each answer.*

1. Who might have introduced the dingo into the country?
2. What main factor decides where the dingo can live in a desert?
3. In what three ways is a dingo different to a domesticated dog?
4. What determines how big an area they live in?
5. What animal might the dingo have helped wipe out?
6. What is the life expectancy of a dingo?
7. When is it better to have a dingo as a pet?
8. Many people are very angry because they regard the dingo as what?

Flexible keywords - Flexible thinking

As you have already seen, some of the keywords you pick will stay the same and are the words you find in the text. However, it is also possible to find synonyms and even antonyms (opposite meaning) of the keyword. Remember **lost** and **saved** seen earlier?

It is important to develop your flexibility in scanning when looking for keywords. Take as an example, Question 4 in the text about the dingo. The question states, "What determines how big an area they live in?" but the answer was found in the sentence stating that it, "varies according to the food supply". Keywords are a little difficult to choose for this question but the word, **determine** is useful if you know other ways of expressing this idea.

It is not uncommon to have similar questions, with similar phrases, in the IELTS test and so the following list will be useful as they all have similar meanings and can all be used in similar ways.

Determine ...

determines / determined by	depends on	decided by
a range of	varies according to	a range of factors
an assortment of	three ways to	a variety of reasons
in several ways	caused by	the situation
leads to	two different types of	due to

Other examples of how this list can help are Questions 2 and 3 of the dingo text. Look at these two questions again and see how the information has been altered in the text.

Now look at a different type of paragraph and answer the two questions that follow.

The Northern Lights

The connection between the Northern Lights and sunspot activity has been suspected since about 1880. Thanks to research conducted since the 1950's, we now know that electrons and protons from the sun are blown towards the earth on the 'solar wind'. 1957-58 was International Geophysical Year and the atmosphere was studied extensively with balloons, radar, rockets and satellites. Rocket research is still conducted by scientists at Poker Flats, a facility under the direction of the University of Alaska at Fairbanks.

Questions 1 - 2

Answer the questions below.

*Choose **NO MORE THAN THREE WORDS** from the passage for each answer.*

1   What was investigated using a variety of methods?
2   We can infer from the passage that sunspot activity releases what?

Remember: infer means to come to a conclusion based on the information that you have been given but with the answer not being stated directly. There would usually be no more than one question like this in the whole test. Notice that although this question type usually has answers in order this particular example about the northern lights has answers out of order. This is possible and can happen in the test.

2 - Sentence Completion

Here you have to complete a number of unfinished sentences by adding a word or short phrase from the text. The number of words you are allowed to use will be stated in the instructions, so make sure you read them carefully.

Very occasionally, you will have to change the grammar of the word or phrase you have chosen to make it fit the sentence. Usually, however, if you select the correct word or words from the text the grammar will also be correct. The words you need to use to complete an answer will usually be from consecutive words (words that are next to each other) and not from words that are in different parts of the text.

Read the short paragraph below and answer the two questions that follow.

Sea-otters worth 700 million in carbon credits

Want to slow global warming? Save a sea otter. So says Chris Wilmers at the University of California, Santa Cruz, whose team has calculated that the animals remove at least 0.18 kilograms of carbon from the atmosphere for every square metre of occupied coastal waters. That means that if sea otters were restored to healthy populations along the coasts of North America they could collectively lock up a mammoth 10^{10} kg of carbon – currently worth more than $700 million on the European carbon-trading market.

Questions 1 - 2

Complete the sentences below.

*Choose **NO MORE THAN ONE WORD AND/OR A NUMBER** from the passage for each answer.*

1 Increasing the otter population might be a way to reduce the amount of _____ in the atmosphere.

2 The amount of carbon that a restored population of otters could remove would be worth over _____.

Now look at the text on Cuba's organic revolution and answer the questions that follow.

Cuba's Organic Revolution

Organic agriculture has been adopted as the official government strategy for all new agriculture in Cuba, after its highly successful introduction just seven years ago. In less than a decade the use of chemical pesticides has dropped by 80%.

The catalyst which revolutionised the Cuban approach, was economic necessity after the collapse of the Soviet Union. Now the island is self-sufficient in organic fruit and vegetables, and organic livestock is also being reared successfully.

Even cabbage, which could not be grown in the past, because it was impossible to control the diamond black moth, now has yields of 60 tonnes per hectare without using fertilisers or pesticides.

To meet the demands of a more labour intensive system of agriculture, the Cuban government has increased rural wages and is providing favourable housing for farm workers which also helps solve the problem of severe housing shortages and overcrowding in the cities. It is also making available abandoned land in urban areas for local communities to farm.

In one co-operative, 40 members are providing food for their own families, with plenty of surplus to provide for community elders, invalids and day care centres. Over 40 countries were represented at a recent Pesticide Action Network (PAN) conference in Cuba to challenge the view that pesticides are essential for agriculture.

The Cuban experience added strength to their conviction that organic agriculture has a great deal to offer and has been unjustifiably ignored by agricultural researchers

Questions 1 - 6

Complete the sentences below.

*Choose **NO MORE THAN THREE WORDS AND/OR A NUMBER** from the passage for each answer.*

1 Cuba has used organic farming for _____.
2 The fall of the Soviet Union created an _____ to grow food.
3 The cultivation of cabbage was made possible after the _____ was killed.
4 Encouraging the development of agriculture has helped reduce _____.
5 A conference in Cuba promoted the view that pesticides were not _____ in farming.
6 _____ should focus more on organic farming.

Now look at the longer reading passage on Japanese Samurai and European Knights and answer the questions that follow.

The Samurai of Japan and European Knights

Japanese and European medieval societies developed along similar feudal lines and in both, a warrior elite emerged as the dominant force. In both parts of the world, honour played an important part in their cultures, and knights and samurai were expected to follow their respective warrior codes, the 'Chivalric Code' in Europe and 'Bushido' (way of the warrior) in Japan.

The codes were not set in stone, they differed from one clan or country to the next and changed down the ages; however there were several key factors in each that tended to be considered essential parts of the way a warrior should conduct his life.

In both Europe and Japan throughout the Middle Ages the sword was considered the most noble weapon, and would contain spiritual significance to the warrior. The samurai famously believed that the legendary samurai sword contained its owner's soul and according to Richard Cohen in his book, 'By the Sword', the same sort of importance was put on the medieval knight's sword, which was believed to possess the essence of the warrior's inner power and true nobility.

One of the main influences for this tradition in Europe was the poem 'Beowulf', who's sword 'Hrunting' would not allow its user to perform evil acts. Before battle, a knight would kiss the cross of his sword on the hilt in an act of religious significance made more so as this part of the sword often contained relics.

Warriors from both regions had similar ideas about how a battle should be fought and it was generally agreed that charging into an enemy, then engaging in one-on-one combat was the noblest way to fight. Although both preferred to fight in a 'gentlemanly' manner, this probably happened much more in fictitious accounts of warfare than on the real battlefield as the realities of war usually would not allow for formalities. Steve Turnbull highlights a case of this in his book, 'Samurai – A Military History'.

During the 'Gempei War' (1180-1185), in the 'Battle of Kurikara', part of the Minamoto force engaged their vastly more powerful enemy, the Taira Clan, in a battle that was conducted in a formal and gentlemanly way. They started with an archery duel, followed by combat between small groups fighting one-on-one and then a pitch battle between one hundred warriors from each side. But the Minamoto had been keeping their enemy occupied and soon the realities of war returned. The Minamoto charged a heard of oxen with flaming pine torches attached to their horns into the Taira, driving them into a valley where they were trapped and subsequently slaughtered. The chronicle the 'Heike Monogatari' states;

> "Thus did seventy thousand horsemen of the Taira perish, buried in this one deep valley; the mountain streams ran with their blood and the mound of their corpses was like a small hill; and in this valley, it is said, there can be seen the marks of arrow and swords even to this day".

Both these codes helped to shape the ideals and values of their people. However, both often differed considerably in what they deemed honourable, suggesting that the definition of the word honour changed to suit the needs of the people involved in a given time and place. To the medieval knight, a defeated enemy of high social rank was to be captured and ransomed when possible but those of low birth could be slaughtered.

To the Japanese, warriors were in battle to die and would be killed without mercy, whereas peasants were not warriors so there was no honour in taking their lives. To take an opposing warrior captive would be to take his honour from him so rather than be taken prisoner, a samurai would take his own life in a ritual known as 'Seppuku', an action that would not only lead to dishonour for the European Christian knight, but also to eternal damnation.

Questions 1 - 7

Complete the sentences below.

***Choose NO MORE THAN THREE WORDS AND/OR A NUMBER** from the passage for each answer.*

1   Both Japanese samurai and Medieval knights valued the importance of _____.
2   The sword in both Japan and Europe was said to be a _____.
3   Knights would _____ their sword before going into battle.
4   The idea of fighting like a gentleman was probably more _____ than real.
5   The Minamoto slaughtered _____ during the Gempei War.
6   The meaning of honour for both the Samurai and European knights _____.
7   A samurai would rather commit _____ than be captured by the enemy.

3 - Summary Completion

In this particular question type you are asked to complete a summary of the text.

Two types of summary

Type One – You have to choose the correct answer from the text. It is very unlikely that you have to take the words you use for one answer from different places in the text. The words should be found together and in one sentence.

This type of summary is not really very different from the sentence completion question type. You can think of a type one summary as nothing more than a paragraph made up of a number of sentence completion type questions. The approach to answering these questions is the same.

Type Two – You have to choose the correct words from a preselected list. The words you select might be different from the words in the text but the meaning of the completed sentence will be the same. Other words, often very similar in meaning, or grammatically incorrect, might be added to confuse you.

As answers are usually in order for both types of summary, you can start completing the summary in any part of the text. Therefore, it is a good idea to look for keywords that can easily be seen in the reading passage and answer these parts first.

Summary Type One - Answers from the text

Look at the short paragraph about Siberian tigers and then complete the summary that follows. Remember that after completion the grammar must be correct and the meaning of the summary must be the same as in the text.

The Siberian Tiger

The Siberian tiger can be found in what was the USSR and seems to live mainly on the lower slopes of mountains. It likes to eat wild boar, wapiti and moose and will travel long distances in search of food. The male tiger weighs more than the female and is bigger than any other species of tiger. Genetically it is closely linked to the now extinct Caspian tiger. Although brown bears are capable of killing tigers, they make up approximately 8% of their diet. Russian conservatives are trying to protect Siberian tigers because they keep the wolf population under control.

Questions 1 - 4

Complete the summary below.

Choose **NO MORE THAN TWO WORDS** *from the passage for each answer.*

The main habitat of the Siberian tiger is in low mountainous areas of the former **1**_____. It hunts a variety of animals including **2**_____. It is similar genetically to the **3**_____. Russian conservatives want to **4**_____ the number of wolves by protecting the Siberian tiger.

Now look at the article about Avebury and answer the eight questions that follow on page 40.

AVEBURY

It is only during the Saxon period that any evidence of a village at Avebury began to appear. When the monuments were enjoying their golden age, the beginnings of the village we now know lay over 3,000 years in the future. The builders of the henge could never have imagined the controversy that the result of their labour was to create amongst the later inhabitants of the area, and the treatment it was to receive, as a result of religious zeal and financial gain. The effect the village was to have on the more recent history of the monuments, adds considerably to the fascination of the Avebury story.

Although a large portion of Avebury village now lies within the henge, throughout the period that the village has existed, the disposition of its buildings has changed. The village of the early Saxon period appears to have lain further to the west, traces of its buildings still being visible today between the present village and the hamlet of Avebury Trusloe. As the village grew, its buildings approached and eventually spread into the interior of the henge itself.

It wasn't until the last century that the historical value of Avebury came to be fully appreciated, when Alexander Keiller began to reveal what lay hidden beneath the ground. At this point the history of the village was to change dramatically as the henge, with the help of its owners, was to fight back against the suffering it had endured at the hands of the earlier villagers. The past began to override the future, when it was deemed expedient to remove many of the buildings that now existed within its confines. Most of the displaced inhabitants were to be re-located to Avebury Trusloe.

It is believed that Keiller's intention was to ultimately remove all modern buildings from within the henge, but when WW2 intervened, and his work at Avebury came to an end, this dramatic and controversial change was never to be completed. The buildings that remain within the henge now, exist in a juxtaposition with the stones that serve to emphasise the remoteness of the culture that built the monument.

The village itself holds much of interest including the church of St. James which has a long history going back to Saxon times. Within is a rare example of a medieval rood-loft once hidden but rediscovered in 1810. It also contains a notable font believed to be of Saxon origin and later adorned with some interesting carvings during the Norman period.

There is also a fine manor house, alongside which is the Alexander Keiller Museum. This contains detailed information regarding the archaeology of the monuments and has many fascinating artefacts from the area on display. Supplementing the Keiller museum is the Barn Gallery which also contains some interesting "hands on" exhibits and other information supplied by the National Trust under whose care the monuments now fall.

Questions 1 - 8

Complete the summary below.

*Choose **NO MORE THAN TWO WORDS AND/OR A NUMBER** from the passage for each answer.*

The village at Avebury dates back to the **1**_____, a time that came many years after the construction of **2**_____. The original village was located outside of the existing monuments but is still **3**_____. When the true importance of Avebury was shown by Alexander Keiller, many villagers were forced to move to **4**_____. However, his plan to clear the henge of everything was thwarted by **5**_____. Although younger than the henge, the village is home to many interesting things. Of particular interest is the **6**_____ found two centuries ago in St. James's church. Norman carvings can also be found there. The Alexander Keiller Museum, found next to the **7**_____, offers detailed **8**_____ information.

Summary Type Two - Answers from the preselected list

Look at the short paragraph about Siberian tigers (seen earlier on page 38) and then complete the summary that follows by picking words from the box. Remember that after completion the grammar must be correct and the meaning of the summary must be the same as the text.

The Siberian Tiger

The Siberian tiger can be found in what was the USSR and seems to live mainly in low mountainous areas. It likes to eat wild boar, wapiti and moose and will travel long distances in search of food. The male tiger weighs more than the female and is bigger than any other species of tiger. Genetically it is closely linked to the now extinct Caspian tiger. Although brown bears are capable of killing tigers, they make up approximately 8% of their diet. Russian conservatives are trying to protect Siberian tigers because they keep the wolf population under control.

Questions 1 - 4

Complete the summary using the list of words, A-I, below.

The main habitat of the Siberian tiger is in low mountainous **1**_____. The female is **2**_____ than the opposite sex. The Caspian tiger is **3**_____ genetically to the Siberian tiger. Russian conservatives are **4**_____ the Siberian tiger and at the same time reducing the wolf population.

A bigger	B closely	C protect
D close	E area	F heavier
G protecting	H lighter	I regions

Now look at the article about Roman remains and answer the seven questions that follow.

Roman Remains

During 2004 – 5 York Archaeological Trust excavated 80 burials in York, in advance of housing developments. The site was part of a large cemetery on the outskirts of the Roman town, across the river from the legionary fortress.

The burials are dated to between the early 2nd century to the late 3rd century, and probably cover most of the period of Roman occupation in northern England (about AD70-410). Almost all are male, and the vast majority are adults – not the usual demographics for a Roman cemetery.

However, despite the evidence for a harsh lifestyle and a violent death, these people had been carefully buried. There was also evidence that funerary feasting had taken place at the cemetery; this often occurred on the anniversary of the death of loved ones.

Were these people gladiators, who were both revered (as superstars) and reviled (as associated with death)? Or were they people who had been executed but given a decent burial? How about soldiers who had died in battle? Or was this evidence of a group of people who had unusual views on religion or burial practices?

As Kurt Hunter Mann, who is leading the research at York Archaeological Trust explains, there is evidence to support other theories, too: "There are numerous pieces of evidence that point towards or are consistent with the interpretation that the skeletons are Roman gladiators, but there is also other evidence that suggest the individuals could have been soldiers, criminals, or members of a religious cult," he says.

One of the most significant pieces of evidence supporting the 'gladiator' conclusion is a large carnivore bite mark – probably inflicted by a lion, tiger or bear, which archaeologists believe may have been sustained in an arena context.

Other evidence includes a high incidence of substantial arm asymmetry – a feature mentioned in ancient Roman literature in connection with a gladiator; some healed and unhealed weapon injuries; possible hammer blows to the head (a feature attested as a probable gladiatorial *coup de grâce* at another gladiator cemetery at Ephesus in Turkey).

Questions 1 - 7

Complete the summary using the list of words, A-L, below.

The area was being dug up as part of a new housing development when a **1**_____ burial ground was discovered. Unlike other Roman sites, this one consists mainly of adults and dates to the time of the Roman occupation in the **2**_____ of England. It is not clear who they were but they could have been soldiers who had been killed when **3**_____ or people with different **4**_____ views. Another theory is that they were **5**_____. A large bite found on one of the skeletons, made by some kind of **6**_____, supports this idea. Some **7**_____ suggest that their cause of death was delivered by the victor of a fight.

A	animal	B	religion	C	fighting	D	gladiators
E	head	F	large	G	lion	H	north
I	religious	J	northern	K	skulls	L	battle

4 - Multiple Choice

In a multiple choice type question, each question has three or four possible answers to choose from but only one of them is correct.

However, you might find a question type where you have to pick two or more answers from the same set of answers. Each correct answer gets one point. Read the instructions carefully so that you know which type of question you are dealing with.

Sir Isaac Newton and Alchemy

Sir Isaac Newton is most famous for the quantification of gravitational attraction, discovering that white light is actually a mixture of immutable spectral colours, and the formulation of calculus. However it is less well documented that Newton spent 30 years engaged in the study of the mysterious art of alchemy, or as it was more commonly known then, chymistry.

Only a tiny fraction of Newton's work on alchemy has been published but he wrote around a million words on the subject, including laboratory notes, indexes of alchemical substances and transcripts from other sources. On his death in 1727, Newton had over 100 manuscripts filled with alchemical material, sold by auctioneers Sotheby as part of a larger collection in 1936. This side of Newton was often an embarrassment to his admirers. His first biographer, John Conduitt, like many commentators who followed, played down the role of alchemy (and other pursuits) in Newton's work, stating;

> "When he was tired with his severer studies his only relief and amusement was going to some other as History and Chronology or Divinity and Chymistry".

Just how important the study of alchemy was to Newton only began to be recognised in 1947, when John Maynard Keynes, who bought much of the work from Sotheby, declared in his essay, 'Newton, the Man'; "Newton was not the first of the age of reason. He was the last of the magicians".

Questions 1 - 4

*Choose the correct letter, **A**, **B**, or **C**.*

1   Newton realised that white light was made up of different what?

    A   colours
    B   mixtures
    C   immutable

2   What was alchemy originally called?

    A   mysterious
    B   chymistry
    C   an art

3   Many thought Newton was what?

    A   tired
    B   an embarrassment
    C   admired

4   What did Keynes call Newton?

    A   old
    B   reasonable
    C   a magician

Now look at the reading passage about ants and aphids and answer the questions that follow.

Ants secrete aphid tranquilizer from their feet

Ants and aphids are known to have a complex relationship. The aphids provide the ants with a food source - the sugar-rich honeydew they excrete when eating plants - and, in return, the ants protect the aphids from ladybirds and other insects that prey on them.

To ensure a constant supply of honeydew, some ant species cultivate large numbers of aphids, and prevent them from straying too far from the colony by biting and damaging, or even completely removing, their wings. The ants also secrete a chemical from their mandibles which inhibits wing development in juvenile aphids.

Ants communicate with each other using a large repertoire of chemical signals, which are actively secreted onto surfaces from exocrine glands on the legs. These signals can recruit nest-mates to food sources, and are also used to mark a colony's territory. Ants secrete chemicals passively too. As an ant moves, hydrocarbons are shed from the cuticle (the waterproof outer lining of the exoskeleton), leaving a chemical trail.

Ants use behavioural signals called semiochemicals to manipulate aphids' nervous systems. (Ant's own behaviour can be manipulated too, by parasitic fungi.) Earlier work had shown that the presence of ants can somehow tranquilize aphids and limit their motor functions, but whether or not this required direct contact between the ants and aphids was unclear.

Using digital video cameras to measure their walking speeds, Tom Oliver of Imperial College London, and colleagues from Royal Holloway and the University of Reading have now shown that aphids move much more slowly on paper that had previously been walked on by ants than on plain paper. They believe that the chemicals laid down in the ants' footprints are used to maintain an aphid "farm" near the ant colony.

Maintaining a populous aphid farm in a small area is obviously beneficial to the ants, as it would provide them with large quantities of honeydew. However, the relationship between the two species is complex, and it seems that the ants' manipulation of the aphids' behaviour is exploitative.

Normally, aphids wander off to new locations when conditions become crowded, to establish new populations nearby. And although ant-attended aphid populations are bigger and live longer than those not attended by ants, the ants prevent the aphid dispersal that is necessary to maintain a stable meta-population, and makes the aphids more vulnerable to parasites.

Questions 1 - 5

*Choose the correct letter, **A**, **B**, **C** or **D**.*

1 How do ants ensure they have regular supplies of honeydew?

    A they damage their wings
    B aphids are made to secrete a chemical
    C they find more juvenile aphids
    D they bite their legs

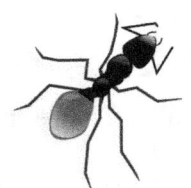

2 How do ants affect aphids' nervous systems?

    A by using parasitic fungi
    B by touching their legs
    C by making a noise
    D by using chemicals

3 When do aphids walk more slowly?

    A when they walk on paper
    B when they are with other aphids
    C when they are on video
    D when they walk on chemicals secreted by ants

4 How can we best describe the relationship between the ants and aphids?

    A beneficial
    B win – win
    C exploitative
    D behavioural

5 What do aphids do if the area becomes overpopulated?

    A start a new colony
    B start a stable meta-population
    C they grow bigger
    D they live longer than ants

Now look at the text on Osiris and answer the questions that follow.

OSIRIS – The Legend

The myth of Osiris the deity has been passed on to us by Plutarch and is therefore well documented. Osiris is the Greek rendering of the Egyptian *Ousir*. Originally he was a nature god and embodied the spirit of vegetation and the ebb and flow of the Nile, as one might expect, but later became worshipped as the god of the dead.

Myth has it that he was born in Thebes of Geb and Nut who ascended to rule the heavens on their death. He was handsome, dark-skinned and taller than other men. When he became King of Egypt he married his sister Isis and immediately taught his people to produce grain and grapes for bread and wine. It was he who created the god cult and built temples and gave law to his people.

He then spread civilisation the world over based on non violence, leaving Isis to rule in his place, but on his return became victim of his evil, jealous brother Set. In the 28th year of his reign Osiris was tricked into a box to meet his death and cast into the Nile. His loving wife immediately set to searching for the box and when it was found hid it whilst their posthumous son Horus was being born. Unfortunately Set found the hiding place and dismembered the body casting it around the kingdom.

Such was her love that Isis resumed the search once more and found every part of Osiris except for the phallus, and with the aid of sorcery brought him back to life. Horus then battled Set and eventually won, and when the gods judged the case they found Osiris to be entirely innocent of all blame and deserving of life once more. However, he preferred to leave Horus as king and depart this earthly life to live in the Elysian Fields where he welcomed the souls of the just. His tomb is said to be in Abydos in the Nile Delta. He was worshipped widely as a trinity with Isis and Horus and was identified with Dionysus and Hades. Isis also took on many other names in other religions such as Demeter, Hera, Selene and even Aphrodite.

Questions 1 - 5

Choose the correct letter, A, B, C or D.

1 What was grain used for?

    A wine
    B bread
    C bread and wine
    D none of the above

2 As a god what did Osiris do?

    A spread the word
    B make his brother jealous
    C encourage civilisation
    D sold grapes

3 Who killed Osiris?

   A King of Egypt
   B Isis
   C Set
   D Horus

4 Who did the son of Osiris fight?

   A Dionysus
   B Set
   C Horus
   D Isis

5 By what name was Isis also known?

   A Demeter
   B Hera
   C Aphrodite
   D all of the above

5 - Table Completion

The task here is to complete a table that summarises some key points from the text. Before starting to answer the questions, it is a good idea to look more closely at the table. The information that is already there will help you with not only the type of answers you are looking for, but also how to write the answer in the answer sheet.

Simply follow whatever style the table is using. For instance, if they supply the name of a person all in capitals, e.g. DAVIS, then do the same. If the table only uses capital letters for the first letter of the name, do the same and so on and so on. The same is also true whenever you complete diagrams and flow charts.

Look at Table A below and look at the style used to write the names and years. Then look at the completed table, Table B, and decide if the answers have been written correctly.

Table A

Name of Author	Birth Date	Name of Book
C. DICKENS	1.	David Copperfield
2.	1908	4. ....
3.	1797	5. ....

Table B

Name of Author	Birth Date	Name of Book
C. DICKENS	1. 1812	David Copperfield
2. I. FLEMING	1908	4. GOLDFINGER
3. M. Shelley	1797	5. Alastor

Many different kinds of information can be found in a table but a common theme is dates and years. Look at the following example of this and try to complete the table.

Changes in Industrial Britain

The spread of railways stimulated communication, and Rowland Hill's standardisation of postal charges in 1839 saw a boom in mail services. But this was nothing compared to the revolution of the telegraph. If you think the Internet is big then just imagine how much bigger it would seem if you had never before seen a computer or telephone. That's what the telegraph was to the Victorians. If rail travel shrank the country, the telegraph crushed it. It opened in the 1840s and soon went stratospheric - within ten years exchanging telegrams had become part of everyday life. By the mid 1860s London was connected with New York and ten years later messages could be exchanged between London and Bombay in minutes.

Questions 1 - 7

Complete the table below.

*Choose **NO MORE THAN TWO WORDS AND/OR A NUMBER** from the passage for each answer.*

Year	Events in Britain
1839	Changes to **1** _____ resulted in an increase in the delivery of mail.
1840s	The beginning of the **2** _____ .
3 _____	You could send messages to **4** _____ .
5 _____	Only **6** _____ for messages to arrive from **7** _____ .

Now look at the reading passage about coeducation and answer the questions that follow.

Single Sex vs. Coeducational High Schools

Female graduates of single-sex high schools demonstrate stronger academic orientations than their coeducational counterparts across a number of different categories, including higher levels of academic engagement, SAT scores, and confidence in mathematical ability and computer skills, according to a UCLA report.

The report's findings, drawn from multiple categories, including self-confidence, political and social activism, life goals, and career orientation, reveal that female graduates of single-sex schools demonstrate greater academic engagement: Nearly two-thirds (62 percent) of single-sex independent school alumnae report spending 11 or more hours per week studying or doing homework in high school, compared with less than half (42 percent) of female graduates of coeducational independent schools.

This research draws data from the annual Freshman Survey, administered by the Cooperative Institutional Research Program at the Higher Education Research Institute at UCLA. The report, which separately considers female students from independent and Catholic high schools nationwide, is based on a comparison of the responses of 6,552 female graduates of 225 private single-sex high schools with those of 14,684 women who graduated from 1,169 private coeducational high schools.

Linda J. Sax, associate professor of education at the UCLA Graduate School of Education & Information Studies and the principal investigator of the study, said: "The generally stronger academic orientations of girls-school alumnae ought to serve them well as they arrive at college, though it remains to be seen whether these advantages are sustained once they are immersed in a coeducational college environment."

Female graduates of single-sex high schools also show higher levels of political engagement, greater interest in engineering careers, measurably more self-confidence in public speaking and a stronger predisposition towards cocurricular engagement.

"The culture, climate and community of girls' schools as a transforming force speaks loud and clear in the results of this study and confirms that at girls' schools it's 'cool to be smart'— there's a culture of achievement in which a girl's academic progress is of central importance, and the discovery and development of her individual potential is paramount," said Meg Milne Moulton, executive director of the National Coalition of Girls' Schools, which commissioned the study. Among the report's key findings was that women who attended single-sex schools tended to outperform their coeducational counterparts: Mean SAT composite scores (verbal plus math) were 43 points higher for female single-sex graduates in the independent school sector and 28 points higher for single-sex alumnae in the Catholic school sector.

Graduates of single-sex schools also enter college with greater confidence in their mathematical and computer abilities. The gap in math confidence is most pronounced in the independent school sector, where 48 percent of female graduates of single-sex independent schools rate their math ability "above average" or in the "highest 10 percent," compared with 37 percent of independent coeducational female graduates.

Confidence in computer skills is also higher among female graduates of single-sex independent schools, with 36 percent rating themselves in the highest categories, compared with 26 percent of female graduates of coeducational independent schools. Additionally, 35 percent of female graduates of single-sex Catholic schools rate their computer skills as "above average" or in the "highest 10 percent," compared with 27 percent of their coeducational counterparts. In an indication of greater, though still low, interest in the field of engineering, alumnae of single-sex independent schools are three times more likely than those from coeducational independent schools to report that they intend to pursue a career in engineering (4.4 percent vs. 1.4 percent).

"Though generally small, many of the favourable outcomes for single-sex alumnae are in areas that have historically witnessed gender gaps favouring men, such as in mathematics, computer science and engineering," Sax said. "Research is needed to clarify whether these benefits are due specifically to gender composition or to the climate and pedagogy that exist in all-girls schools."

Political engagement also is notably higher among female graduates of single-sex independent schools, with 58 percent reporting that it is "very important" or "essential" for them to keep up to date with political affairs, compared with 48 percent of female graduates of coeducational independent schools. Women at single-sex Catholic schools are also more likely than their coeducational counterpart to value political engagement (43 percent, compared with 36 percent).

Graduates of single-sex schools are also more likely than their coeducational counterparts to report that there is a very good chance they will participate in student clubs or groups while in college: 70 percent of single-sex independent school alumnae anticipate involvement in campus organizations, compared with 60 percent of coeducational alumnae.

Female graduates of single-sex independent schools also show more self-confidence in public speaking, with 45 percent rating their public speaking ability "above average" or in the "highest 10 percent," compared with 39 percent of female graduates of coeducational independent high schools.

In addition to providing descriptive comparisons between single-sex and coeducational alumnae, the study also reports on the many ways in which the single-sex effect remains significant after accounting for key differences between these groups in terms of school characteristics (such as enrolment, location and course offerings) and the demographic backgrounds of the women who attend all-girls schools (such as race/ethnicity, family income and parental education).

These results provide further evidence of the role of single-sex education in promoting women's academic and political engagement, confidence in math and computer skills, and interest in engineering careers.

Questions 1 - 9

Complete the tables below.

*Choose **NO MORE THAN THREE WORDS AND/OR A NUMBER** from the passage for each answer.*

	Independent	
	Single Sex	Coeducational
11 hours plus per week studying homework	**1**_____	42%
Number of graduates involved in the research	6,552	**2**_____
Number of private schools	225	**3**_____

Mean SAT scores – single sex - Catholic	**4**_____	
Mean SAT scores – single sex - Independent	**5**_____	
Above average in Math - Independent	48%	**6**_____
Above average in Computer Skills - Independent	36%	**7**_____
Above average in Computer Skills - Catholic	**8**_____	27%
Above average confidence in Speaking - Independent	45%	**9**_____

6 - Labelling Flow Charts / Processes

For this question type you have to fill in the missing information to complete a flow chart or process using information from the text. This is often found in one paragraph but could be spread over a number of different paragraphs. Typically, you will see a step by step analysis of, for example, how something is made.

To start, use the best possible keyword from anywhere in the chart to find the correct paragraph. Look at the example below about the Enigma machine and complete the flow chart that follows. Remember that flow charts (or processes) might not contain all of the steps mentioned in the text.

Enigma Machine

The basic operating procedure of the Enigma machine was simple. To send an encrypted message, the operator set the Enigma's electric and mechanical settings (the plug wirings and the rotor wheels) to a predefined initial combination known to him and to the receiving operator. Then he typed the free text message on the Enigma's keyboard. For each typed letter, a different letter was lit in the upper board. The operator wrote down each lit letter, so that when he finished typing the original message on the Enigma, he had a meaningless stream of letters, which was the Enigma-encrypted message. He then transmitted the encrypted message with a standard Morse code radio transmitter. The receiving operator wrote the received encrypted message, set his Enigma machine to the same predefined combination, and then typed the message at the machine's keyboard. Typing the encrypted message on his Enigma machine with the same combination of settings deciphered it, so that the operator read the original free text message by the letters lit in the upper board as he typed.

Questions 1 - 6

Complete the flow chart below.

*Choose **NO MORE THAN THREE WORDS** for each answer.*

The Operation Procedure

operator sets machine to a **1** _____

types a **2** _____

transmits **3** _____

receiving operator sets **4** _____

types **5** _____

message deciphered

reads original message on **6** _____

Now look at the second example and complete the process that follows.

Doll Restoration

This is a good example of how the average doll collector receives a doll. They will find a beautiful antique doll that does not look as beautiful as it should, but with proper restoration she can be as beautiful as the day she was created. Here, there are two main problems, the eye mechanism has lost its original look, and it has a loose head. We removed the mohair wig and removed the eye system. Then we separated the head from the composition body and chemically cleaned the head, removing old dirt, and wax, but not harming the original art work. We repaired the missing porcelain teeth by making duplicate porcelain teeth to match, and reinserted them. Then we took the original eye system, and reconditioned it. We then did the waxing of the eye mechanism and reset the eye bar so the eye bar would open and close as it originally did. What a wonderful difference. At this point we only had to chemically clean and restyle the original mohair wig. Our seamstress took over at this point with suggestions from the owner on likes and dislikes using original period clothing designs. She now looked, I'm sure, very much as she would have originally looked the day a little child fell in love with her for the first time.

Questions 1 - 11

Complete the flow chart below.

*Choose **NO MORE THAN THREE WORDS** for each answer.*

Two main problems

1 _____   2 _____

3 _____ two parts of the doll

4 _____   5 _____

6 _____ the head

removed 7 _____ and _____

made duplicate 8 _____

reconditioned 9 _____ and mechanism

10 _____ mohair wig

dressed doll in authentic 11 _____ clothes

53

Now complete the third flow chart after looking at the text.

Salmon

The female salmon lay up to about 5000 eggs in freshwater, in a process called spawning. These eggs are protected in a little hollow, or rudd, at the bottom of a river and are covered in gravel until they hatch. Due to the exhausting journey the adult salmon have made from the ocean, they usually die a few days after mating. Many eggs will fail to hatch and might even be eaten by predators. However, some will survive and grow into alevin. Food is initially supplied from the yolk in the egg and will stay attached to the alevin even after it has left the egg. Once all of the nutrition has been taken from the yolk, the alevin turn into fry, about 800 in total. Much of their time is then spent trying to avoid predators as they are still very small and vulnerable. Fry might stay in freshwater for up to three years but then begin their long and tiring journey to the sea. To adapt to life in salt water the fry go through a transition called smolting and turn into approximately 200 smolt from the original 5000 eggs. After arriving in the sea the young adults turn into mature adults – about 10 in all – and remain in the sea for between one to five years. They then swim back to the same river where they were born to find a mate and lay eggs.

Questions 1 - 7

Complete the flow chart below.

Choose **NO MORE THAN TWO WORDS AND/OR A NUMBER** *for each answer.*

Life Cycle of a Salmon

female salmon lay 1 _____

   the eggs are laid in 2 _____

     in a few days adults 3 _____

       alevin feed on 4 _____

         many fry are eaten by 5 _____

           smolt are able to live in 6 _____

             adults stay in the sea for up to 7 _____

               they return to lay eggs in the place they were first born

Now look at a longer reading passage and complete the diagram that follows.

Memory

We'll begin our discussion of memory with a comprehensive and influential model of how human memory works. The model is called the modal model and was developed by Atkinson and Shiffrin (1968) to describe how information is encoded, stored, and retrieved from memory. The model is not the only one proposed and models have since become even more complex and specific, but this model will help you understand some of the important processes that are part of our memory, as well as introduce some of the major terms and concepts important for understanding how memory works.

The first part of the model involves sensory input from the environment in the form of stimuli that we encounter in our everyday lives. For example, suppose that you are having a conversation with a friend. Your senses automatically register everything in the environment in different ways. You can hear what your friend is saying to you, the cars passing by the street, and the chirps of the birds flying overhead. You can see your friend standing in front of you, the people passing by behind, and the building even further in the distance. You can smell the mulch in the planter, your friend's cologne, and the sawdust from a construction site.

All of this information is registered in sensory stores, each compartmentalized by mode: visual, auditory and haptic, according to Atkinson and Shiffrin. These sensory stores hold the information for a very short period of time (e.g., a few seconds) and then the information is either sent to a short-term store or disappears to make room for new information as it comes in. This is necessary, because we are constantly bombarded with new information and if this was all stored in our memory for more than a few seconds, we would quickly run out of storage space. Information that gets processed in some way (e.g., we pay particular attention to it or we rehearse it) is forwarded from the sensory stores to the short-term store. This also has a limited capacity, but the capacity can be increased by storing information in different ways (e.g., organization strategies).

The short-term store can hold information for up to about a minute, but this time limit can also be increased by certain techniques (e.g., rehearsal). For example, suppose you call the operator for a phone number you want. The operator gives you the phone number, but you have nothing to write it on before you redial. What do you do? Well, one obvious strategy is to repeat the number to yourself over and over. You are rehearsing the number and keeping it in the short-term store until you need to dial it (called response output from the short-term store).

If you were to rehearse the number for a long time, it might get stored in a more permanent place in memory called the long-term store. According to Atkinson and Shiffrin, the long-term store is the place in our memory where information can be held for long periods of time (minutes up to many years). This does not mean that information can always be accessed from the long-term store.

There are many factors that contribute to our ability to retrieve memories. According to the model though, to retrieve information, it must be accessed from the long-term store and moved into the short-term store for a response output. This process can be aided or impeded, depending on the way in which we try to retrieve the memory. But because the retrieval process involves moving the information back to the short-term store, a response needs to be made within about a minute or else it will be lost from your memory.

Questions 1 - 12

Complete the flow chart below.

*Choose **NO MORE THAN THREE WORDS AND/OR A NUMBER** for each answer.*

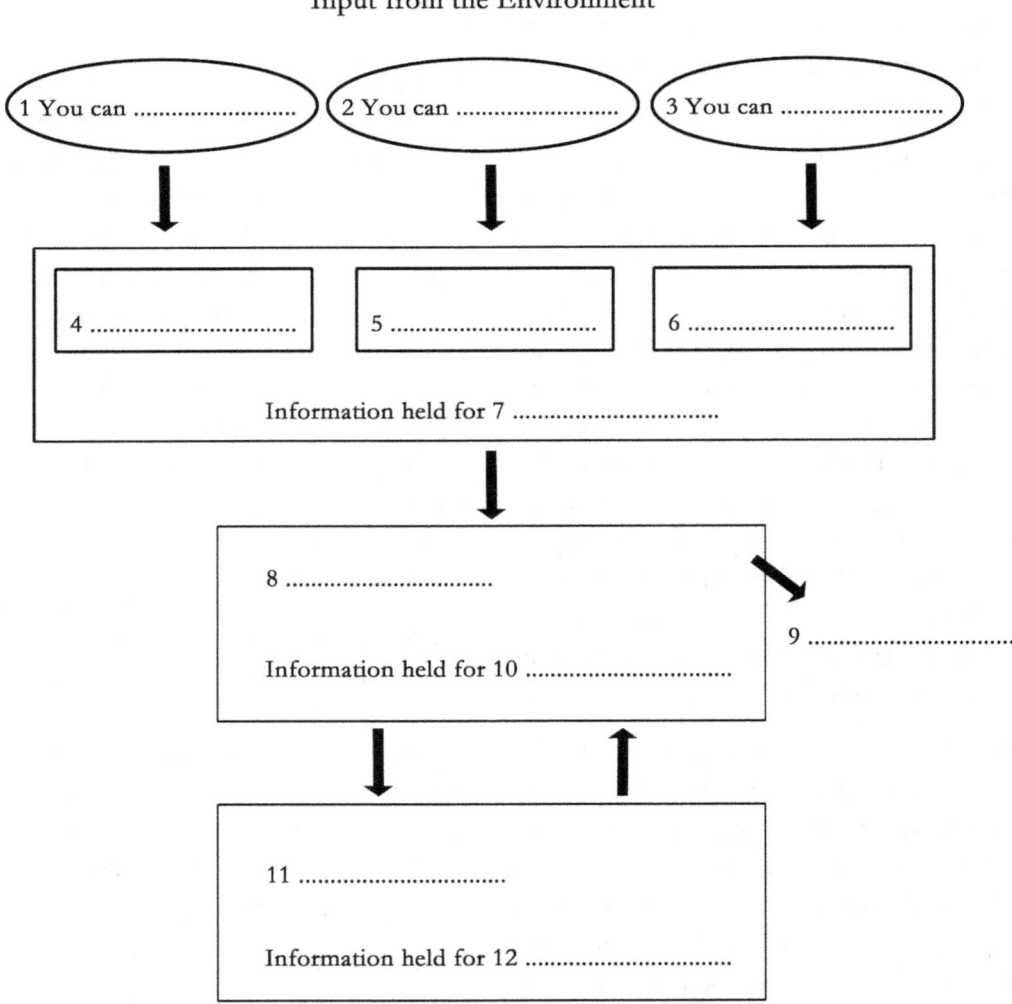

7 - Matching

Here you have to pair up pieces of information to form a perfect match. For example, you might have to:

1. Match the names of different people with what they said.

2. Match the names of different people and what they did.

3. Match the two halves of different sentences together.

The Origin of Language

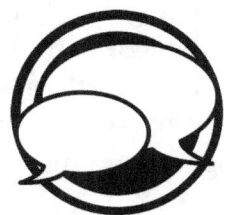

The question of the origin of language is one that has been raised and discussed repeatedly at least since the eighteenth century. Before that it was supposed that language must have been part of God's gift to Adam. There was a tradition of linguistic inquiry that sought to discover what original tongue it was that Adam spoke, but the question of how he came to be able to speak at all was not really raised.

In the eighteenth century, especially in France, the idea that human characteristics could be accounted for by nature rather than by Divine gift was widely discussed, and such figures as Rousseau, Condillac and Maupertuis, among others, attempted to show that language could have had natural beginnings or could have been invented by natural reason. There were some who countered this - for example, the Lutheran pastor Sussmilch who, in 1756, attempted to refute the arguments of Maupertuis that language was an invention by showing that its intricate, and systematic, patterning could not be the product of human reason alone but must have been the creation of God.

However, it was the German philosopher Herder who in 1772 won the competition set by the Berlin Academy of Sciences with an essay that refuted all arguments for a Divine origin of language. For a long time his statement was considered to have settled the question.

The nineteenth century saw the development of historical linguistics and, for a time, this seemed to give new life to the question of language origins. It was found that careful and systematic comparison of related languages could lead to a reconstruction of older languages of which they were descendants. In particular, much effort was expended in the reconstruction of Indo-European, the language proposed as ancestral to many languages of Europe and to some of India. For a time it was thought that such historical work could lead to an understanding of the nature of earlier forms of language and perhaps, eventually, to an insight into its earliest form.

However, it soon became apparent that this was impossible. In reconstructing the ancestors of languages presently spoken it was realized that all you could do was to reconstruct versions of language which, though precedents for contemporary forms, were no different in principle from those that could be directly observed. It was realized that such reconstructions, whatever they might tell us about how specific languages change with time, could throw no light on the issue of how language came about in the first place.

Furthermore, as historical work proceeded and more and more languages were carefully examined, it appeared that the changes languages undergo with time, though to some degree lawful, were neither consistent nor progressive. It was not found, for instance, that older languages were simpler than contemporary languages, nor was it found possible to show that any of the various types of language proposed — such as 'isolating', 'agglutinating' or 'inflecting' — represented earlier or later stages in language development. In other words, the changes that languages were found to undergo with time were manifestly not to be accounted for by any clear process of evolution. The practitioners of historical linguistics, accordingly, abandoned any quest for a general theory of language development, and they gave up the idea that their work could throw light on language origins.

By the end of the first decade of the twentieth century, the emphasis in linguistics had shifted from historical analysis to the analysis of the synchronic structure of languages. De Saussure's argument that historical (diachronic) analysis was not relevant for understanding the organization of a given linguistic system when considered in its use by a community of speakers, had an important influence. In addition, Franz Boas and his pupil Edward Sapir, working in North America, showed that the languages of the Native Americans had to be understood in their own terms, since they had grammars and sound systems that could not be comprehended in terms of systems derived from European languages.

This work helped to show that the languages of so-called 'primitive' peoples were just as complicated as the most sophisticated and modern of European languages, and that there was no evidence for the preservation of earlier forms of language. The development of methods for describing the diversity of human languages became a major preoccupation for linguistics, and questions about the origin of the human capacity for language, or of how languages had evolved from earlier forms to those of the present, seemed less and less relevant. Speculation about language origins thus appeared worthless, for there was no evidence on which it could be based. Anyone's guess was as good as another's. The wastepaper baskets of London were perhaps, after all, the best destination for such imaginings.

Questions 1 - 3

Look at the following statements and the list of people below.

Match each statement with the correct person.

1 Felt that historical analysis was irrelevant.

2 Believed that it was impossible for all languages to be explained with one system.

3 Felt that human language was Divine.

List of People
A   Condillac
B   Boas
C   Herder
D   Sussmilch
E   De Saussure

Questions 4 - 9

*Complete each sentence with the correct ending, **A-F**, below.*

4 Insights into the earliest form of the Indo-European language

5 A comparative study of similar languages

6 A philosopher

7 Language before the 18th Century

8 An "unsophisticated" language

9 A study into the evolution of language

A	was recognised for his views on the Divine origin of language.
B	was seen to be as complex as any modern language.
C	was a way to better understand their ancestral languages.
D	was impossible.
E	was thought of as Adams gift from God.
F	was seen as pointless.

The Penny Black

In 1840, the United Kingdom introduced the penny black, the first adhesive postage stamp issued anywhere in the world.

For many years the postal service in the U.K. had been a very expensive service for ordinary people to use. The costs were prohibitive, a single letter sometimes costing a working person's full day's wage. The postal system also had many strange anomalies, such as certain categories of mail going free (and being therefore paid for by the charges on others), newspapers going for nothing, most mail being paid for by the addressee rather than by the sender, and so on.

There were moves for postal reform for many years, until eventually these moves started gathering some force through the attention of many, amongst whom Rowland Hill is the best known, and Robert Wallace, MP for Greenock, was instrumental. The story is long and involved, but eventually The Penny Postage Bill was passed by Parliament on 17 August 1839. Some basic elements of the plan were the lowering of postage rates for basic letters to one penny, the removal of certain idiosyncrasies, that prepayment would become normal, and the availability of printed envelopes, letter sheets, and labels to show prepayment. The "labels" were the penny black and twopence blue.

A bookseller and printer from Dundee, James Chalmers, holds a strong claim to be the actual inventor of the adhesive postage stamp. He is said to have been interested in postal reform from about 1822, and to have printed samples of his idea for printed gummed labels in August 1834. It seems that, although Hill also presented the idea of adhesive stamps, he was probably keener on the use of standard prepaid letter folders, such as were issued in 1840 using a design by William Mulready.

The new stamps went on sale on 1st May 1840, and were valid for postage from 6th May 1840 (although some were used during the 1st-5th May period). The Mulreadies were issued at the same time. Public reaction to these new items was quite the opposite to Rowland Hill's expectations. The labels were well-received and admired; the Mulready design was lambasted and ridiculed. Initial supplies of the stamps were rushed through the printing and distribution process, but supplies soon caught up with requirements.

The stamps were printed in sheets of 240, engraved on steel plates, on gummed paper with a single small crown watermark on each stamp. Eleven different printing plates were used, and it is possible in almost every case to work out which plate any individual stamp was printed from by little characteristics. Things like the positioning of the corner letters within their squares, the presence of the "O flaw", which rays of the stars in the upper corners are broken at what points, and so on, can point to a correct plate identification, but more specialised literature is required in order to do this. Some plates are scarcer than others, plate 11 being the scarcest.

Every penny black stamp has letters in the lower two corners. These simply identify what sheet position the stamp occupied. When the printing plates were produced the lower squares were blank, and the letters were punched in by hand.

The left square letter shows which horizontal row the stamp was in - the first row being A, the second B, and so on down to the twentieth row with T. The right square letter indicates the vertical column, again with A for the first column, B, C, and so on across to L for the last (twelfth) column. It should be noted therefore that each letter combination is just as common or as scarce as any other.

There were 68,158,080 penny blacks issued (yes, 68 million!), and even with only a 2% survival rate, there are likely to be about 1.3 million still in existence. The survival rate may well be considerably higher than 2%, as it should be remembered that in 1840 the use of envelopes was unusual, most letters being written, folded, and sealed with sealing wax; this meant that whenever a letter was filed in a lawyer's office, bank, etc., the whole thing would be kept - letter and outer cover including the adhesive stamp

Aspects of condition; physical condition - any fault such as a thin, tear, crease, or stain will lower the value, and the number, size, and regularity of the margins make a big difference to value. The stamps were not perforated, and had to be separated using scissors or a knife. As there was only about 1mm between one stamp and another, it was very easy to stray just a little and cut into the printed design of the stamp. A stamp with two full margins and perhaps a couple of other part margins is about average. Collectors will pay higher prices for examples with four good, wide, and even margins.

Questions 1 - 4

Look at the following people (and organisations) and the list of statements below.

Match each person or organisation with the correct statement.

1   Rowland Hill
2   James Chalmers
3   William Mulready
4   Parliament

	List of Statements
A	Introduced new legislation to lower cost of sending letters
B	Designed a prepaid letter folder
C	Designed the printing plates
D	Preferred prepaid letter folders
E	Interested in postal reforms since the 1830s
F	Probably invented adhesive postage stamps

Questions 5 - 9

*Complete each sentence with the correct ending, **A-G**, below.*

5   After reforms, most mail was

6   Every penny black was

7   Putting a letter in an envelope was

8   Each steel printing plate was

9   Keeping the borders of each stamp was

A	unusual in 1840.
B	able to print sheets of 240 stamps.
C	paid for by the sender.
D	very difficult to achieve.
E	very expensive to send.
F	designed with two letters in the bottom corners.
G	quickly accepted.

8 - Paragraph Selection

In this question type you have to match each statement with a particular paragraph or section in the reading passage. To understand this more clearly, look at four statements, Questions **1-4**, and match them to four paragraphs **A**, **B**, **C** or **D** taken from an article called, "The Unexplained Powers Of Animals".

A
Most research on animal navigation has been carried out with homing pigeons, and this research over many decades has served only to deepen the problem of understanding their direction-finding ability. Navigation is goal-directed, and implies that the animals know where their home is even when they are in an unfamiliar place, and have to cross unfamiliar terrain.

B
Homing pigeons can find their way back to their loft over hundreds of miles of unfamiliar terrain. Migrating European swallows travel thousands of miles to their feeding grounds in Africa, and in the spring return to their native place. Some dogs, cats, horses and other domesticated animals also have a good sense of direction and can make their way home from unfamiliar places many miles away.

C
Pigeons do not know their way home by remembering the twists and turns of the outward journey, because birds taken in closed vans by devious routes find their way home perfectly well, as do birds that have been anaesthetized on the outward journey, or transported in rotating drums. They do not navigate by the sun, because pigeons can fly home on cloudy days and can even be trained to navigate at night. However, they may use the sun as a simple compass to keep their bearings. Although they use landmarks in familiar terrain, they can fly home from unfamiliar places hundreds of kilometres from their home, with no familiar landmarks. They cannot smell their home from hundreds of miles away, especially when it is downwind, although smell may play a part in their homing ability when they are close to familiar territory.

D
Some biologists hope that the homing of pigeons might turn out to be explicable in terms of a magnetic sense. But even if pigeons have a compass-sense (which is not proven), this could not explain their ability to navigate. If you were taken blindfold to an unknown destination and given a compass, you would know where north was, but not the direction of your home.

Questions 1 - 4

Which paragraph contains the following information?

1   navigational ability of pigeons is not easily confused

2   hoped for explanation still poses problems

3   importance of homing pigeons in navigational research

4   an explanation of why pigeons are not unique in their ability to navigate

9 - TRUE, FALSE, NOT GIVEN

The skill needed here is to be able to compare a question sentence with information from the text and decide if it is either true, false, or not given.

As you start to practice this question type, it is important to remember that everything in the text is true. What you have to decide is whether or not the question sentences you are given are also true. If true then you will be able to find a sentence in the text that states the same information. Keywords will help you find the right sentence to read.

To make it more difficult the question sentence will have been changed in some way (paraphrased) to make it harder to see the connection between the two sentences. For instance, look at a short text taken from an article about the conservation of the saiga antelope in Central Asia. Then, answer the four questions that follow. Are they **TRUE**, **FALSE** or **NOT GIVEN**?

The Saiga Antelope

In 1993 more than a million saiga antelope (*Saiga tatarica*) crowded the steppes of Central Asia. However, by 2004 just 30,000 remained, many of them female. The species had fallen prey to relentless poaching - with motorbikes and automatic weapons - in the wake of the Soviet Union's collapse. This 97% decline is one of the most dramatic population crashes of a large mammal ever seen. Poachers harvest males for their horns, which are used in fever cures in traditional Chinese medicine. The slaughter is embarrassing for conservationists. In the early 1990s, groups such as WWF actively encouraged the saiga hunt, promoting its horn as an alternative to the horn of the endangered rhino. "The saiga was an important resource, well managed by the Soviet Union," says John Robinson, at the Wildlife Conservation Society (WCS) in New York City, US. "But with the breakdown of civil society and law and order, that management ceased."

Questions 1 - 4

Do the following statements agree with the information given in the reading passage?

Write:

   TRUE   *if the statement agrees with the information*
   FALSE   *if the statement contradicts the information*
   NOT GIVEN   *if there is no information on this*

1 In the early nineties Central Asia's steppes was home to over one million saiga.
2 This 97% decline is the most dramatic population crash of a large mammal ever seen.
3 Traditional medicine uses the poached horns of male members of the group.
4 The WWF managed to save many rhinos because it encouraged the hunting of saiga.

Small changes make all the difference

As question two about the saiga antelope shows, you must be careful with sentences that seem to be stating the same thing but might change the meaning in some way. Words like – **more than**, **might**, **must** – can either be left out of or put into a sentence and change the meaning. Question two states that, "This 97% decline is **the most** ...". But in the text it states, " **one of the most** ..." and so the answer must be **FASLE**.

For some questions, the text might not have any information connected to a **NOT GIVEN** question (not even keywords). In other situations, keywords might be found but not enough information is given in the text for you to say if the statement is **TRUE** or **FALSE**. Avoid a situation where you spend too long looking for information. It is possible that the answer is **NOT GIVEN**.

Now look at the reading passage on creating synthetic life and answer the questions that follow.

Have Researchers Created Synthetic Life at the J. Craig Venter Institute?

Researchers often insert a gene or two into an organism in order to make it do something unique. For example, researchers inserted the insulin gene into bacteria in order to make them produce human insulin. However, researchers at the J. Craig Venter Institute (JCVI) in Rockville, MD, have now created organisms that contain a completely synthetic genome. This synthetic genome was designed by computer, resulting in the "first self-replicating species ... whose parent is a computer," as stated by Dr. Venter, the lead scientist on this project.

In essence, the JCVI scientists took the genome of one bacterial species, *M. mycoides*, synthesized it from scratch, and then transplanted it into a different bacterial species, *M. capricolum*. The DNA was synthesized as a series of cassettes, or pieces, spanning roughly 1,080 bases (the chemical units that make up DNA) each. These cassettes were then painstakingly assembled together and slowly input into the *M. capricolum* species.

The JVCI researchers also included several "watermarks" in the synthetic genome. Because DNA contains introns, which are non-expressed spans of DNA, as well as exons, which are expressed spans of DNA, much of the code can be altered without affecting the final organism. Also, the four bases of the DNA code - A,C,G, and T - can combine into triplets to code for 20 amino acids (the chemical units of which protein is composed), as well as start and stop instructions for gene expression. These amino acids are designated by single alphabetical letters; for example, tryptophan is designated by the letter W. Thus, by using the amino acid "alphabet," the JCVI researchers were able to insert sequences of DNA that were specifically designed to spell out the names of study authors, project contributors, web addresses, and even include quotations from James Joyce, and Richard Feynman. Such engineering helped clarify that the *M. capricolum* genome is completely synthetic and not a product of natural bacterial growth and replication.

Over one million total bases were inserted into *M. capricolum*. The final result was a bacterial cell that originated from *M. capricolum*, but behaved like and expressed the proteins of *M. mycoides*. This synthetic *M. mycoides* bacterium was also able to self-replicate, a fundamental quality of life.

The demonstration that completely synthetic genomes can be used to start synthetic life promises other exciting discoveries and technologies. For example, photosynthetic algae could be transplanted with genomes that would enable these organisms to produce biofuel. In fact, the ExxonMobil Research and Engineering Company has already worked out an agreement with Synthetic Genomics, the company that helped fund the JCVI research team, to start just such a project.

While some researchers agree that the technical feat of the JCVI team is astounding, detractors point to the difficulty of creating more complicated organisms from scratch. Other researchers point to the fact that some biofuels are already being produced by microorganisms via the genetic engineering of only a handful of genes. And Dr. David Baltimore, a leading geneticist at CalTech, has countered the significance of the work performed by the JCVI research team, stating that its lead researcher, Dr. Venter, "... has not created life, only mimicked it."

Questions 1 - 7

Do the following statements agree with the information given in the reading passage?

Write:

TRUE	*if the statement agrees with the information*
FALSE	*if the statement contradicts the information*
NOT GIVEN	*if there is no information on this*

1 DNA was also injected into animals.

2 Bacteria have been made to produce insulin.

3 Tryptophan is one example of an amino acid.

4 Bacteria were taught to spell.

5 Fuel is already being produced using genetically altered algae.

6 The research team gave money to ExxonMobil.

7 The synthetic bacteria can only replicate for several generations.

Now look at the next reading passage and answer the questions that follow.

Alaskans' vitamin D production slows to a halt

Interested people are needed to participate in a one-year study to assess the effects of long dark winters on the vitamin D and calcium levels of Fairbanks residents.

So began a recruitment poster Meredith Tallas created 25 years ago. Now living in Oakland, California, Tallas was a University of Alaska Fairbanks student in 1983 who wanted to study how levels of a vitamin related to sun exposure fluctuated in people living so far from the equator.

"The most obvious vitamin to study in Alaska is vitamin D, because of the low light in winter," Tallas said recently over the phone from her office in Berkeley.

Forty-seven people responded to Tallas' 1983 request, and her master's project was underway. By looking at the blood work of those Fairbanks residents every month and analyzing their diets, she charted their levels of vitamin D, which our skin magically produces after exposure to a certain amount of sunshine. We also get vitamin D from foods, such as vitamin-D enriched milk and margarine, and fish (salmon are a good source). Vitamin D is important for prevention of bone diseases, diabetes and other maladies.

If you live at a latitude farther north than about 42 degrees (Boston, Detroit, or Eugene, Oregon), the sun is too low on the horizon from November through February for your skin to produce vitamin D, according to the National Institutes of Health. Tallas also saw another potential Alaska limitation on the natural pathway to vitamin D production.

"Most outdoor activity requires covering all but the face and hands approximately seven months of the year," she wrote in her thesis. "During the summer months residents keep much of their bodies clothed because of the persistent and annoying mosquitoes and biting flies and because of this, an Alaskan summer suntan becomes one of the face and hands."

But even over bundled people like Alaskans show signs of enhanced vitamin D production from the sun. Tallas found the highest levels of vitamin D in the Fairbanks volunteers' blood in July, and the lowest levels in March. Tallas attributed the July high occurring about a month after summer solstice to the time needed for the body's processing of sunlight and the conversion to vitamin D.

In Tallas' study, volunteers showed low levels of vitamin D in winter months, but most got sufficient doses of vitamin D from sources other than the sun. Tallas also found that males had an average of 16 percent more vitamin D in their blood throughout the study, which she attributed in part to men being outside more.

In charting an average for people's time outside (you can't convert sunlight to vitamin D through windows), she found December was the low point of sunlight exposure, when sun struck the skin of her volunteers for less than 20 minutes per day. People spent an average of more than two hours exposed to Alaska sunlight in June and July. They seemed to hunker down in October, when time outside in the sun dropped to about half an hour after almost two hours of daily sun exposure in September.

Vitamin D levels in the volunteers' blood dropped in August, September, October, November, December, January, February, and March, but Tallas saw an occasional leap in midwinter. "When someone had gone to Hawaii, we could see, very exactly, a significant spike in their vitamin D levels,"

Tallas said. "The only surprise was how it came a month or two after."

In her thesis, Tallas wrote that a midwinter trip to somewhere close to the equator would be a good thing for boosting Alaskans' vitamin D levels. "Presuming that an individual's lowest circulating vitamin D level is found in March or April, such trips could potentially have a very significant effect in improving late winter vitamin D status," she wrote in her thesis. "Unfortunately a majority of Alaskan residents do not take such trips often." An easy alternative for Alaskans not travelling southward during the winter is eating foods rich in vitamin D or taking vitamin D supplements, Tallas said.

Questions 1 - 9

Do the following statements agree with the information given in the reading passage?

Write:

> **TRUE** *if the statement agrees with the information*
> **FALSE** *if the statement contradicts the information*
> **NOT GIVEN** *if there is no information on this*

1 Tallas wanted to know why the levels of Vitamin D were lower in people from Alaska.

2 Men, women and children volunteered for the study.

3 People in Boston have higher levels of diabetes.

4 Vitamin D levels were found to peak in July.

5 All of the volunteers obtained high enough levels of Vitamin D in the winter.

6 Men had higher levels of Vitamin D.

7 People become depressed in the winter because of the lack of sunlight.

8 Vitamin D levels dropped over eight consecutive months.

9 Many Alaskans go on trips in the winter.

10 - YES, NO, NOT GIVEN

As with the true, false, not given questions, you must compare a question sentence with information from the text and decide if it is either **YES**, **NO** or **NOT GIVEN**.

Coral Triangle

The Philippines is part of the so-called "coral triangle," which spans eastern Indonesia, parts of Malaysia, Papua New Guinea, Timor Leste and the Solomon Islands. It covers an area that is equivalent to half of the entire United States.

Although there are 1,000 marine protected areas (MPAs) within the country, only 20 percent are functioning, the update said. MPAs are carefully selected areas where human development and exploitation of natural resources are regulated to protect species and habitats.

In the Philippines, coral reefs are important economic assets, contributing more than US$1 billion annually to the economy.

"Many local, coastal communities do not understand or know what a coral reef actually is, how its ecosystem interacts with them, and why it is so important for their villages to preserve and conserve it," Southeast Asian Centre of Excellence (SEA CoE) said in a statement.

Unknowingly, coral reefs – touted to be the tropical rainforest of the sea – attract a diverse array of organisms in the ocean. They provide a source of food and shelter for a large variety of species including fish, shellfish, fungi, sponges, sea anemones, sea urchins, turtles and snails.

A single reef can support as many as 3,000 species of marine life. As fishing grounds, they are thought to be 10 to 100 times as productive per unit area as the open sea. In the Philippines, an estimated 10-15 per cent of the total fisheries come from coral reefs.

Not only coral reefs serve as home to marine fish species, they also supply compounds for medicines. The Aids drug AZT is based on chemicals extracted from a reef sponge while more than half of all new cancer drug research focuses on marine organisms.

Unfortunately, these beautiful coral reefs are now at serious risk from degradation. According to scientists, 70 percent of the world's coral reefs may be lost by 2050. In the Philippines, coral reefs have been slowly dying over the past 30 years.

The World Atlas of Coral Reefs, compiled by the United Nations Environment Program (UNEP), reported that 97 percent of reefs in the Philippines are under threat from destructive fishing techniques, including cyanide poisoning, over-fishing, or from deforestation and urbanization that result in harmful sediment spilling into the sea.

Last year, Reef Check, an international organization assessing the health of reefs in 82 countries, stated that only five percent of the country's coral reefs are in "excellent condition." These are the Tubbataha Reef Marine Park in Palawan, Apo Island in Negros Oriental, Apo Reef in Puerto Galera, Mindoro, and Verde Island Passage off Batangas.

About 80-90 per cent of the incomes of small island communities come from fisheries. "Coral reef fish yields range from 20 to 25 metric tons per square kilometre per year for healthy reefs," said Angel C. Alcala, former environment secretary.

Alcala is known for his work in Apo Island, one of the world-renowned community-run fish sanctuaries in the country. It even earned him the prestigious Ramon Magsaysay Award. Rapid population growth and the increasing human pressure on coastal resources have also resulted in the massive degradation of the coral reefs. Robert Ginsburg, a specialist on coral reefs working with the Rosenstiel School of Marine and Atmospheric Science at the University of Miami, said human beings have a lot to do with the rapid destruction of reefs. "In areas where people are using the reefs or where there is a large population, there are significant declines in coral reefs," he pointed out.

"Life in the Philippines is never far from the sea," wrote Joan Castro and Leona D'Agnes in a new report. "Every Filipino lives within 45 miles of the coast, and every day, more than 4,500 new residents are born."

Estimates show that if the present rapid population growth and declining trend in fish production continue, only 10 kilograms of fish will be available per Filipino per year by 2010, as opposed to 28.5 kilograms per year in 2003.

Questions 1 - 5

Do the following statements agree with the information given in the reading passage?

Write:

> *YES*   *if the statement reflects the claims of the writer*
>
> *NO*   *if the statement contradicts the claims of the writer*
>
> *NOT GIVEN*   *if it is impossible to say what the writer thinks about this*

1   The natural resources in twenty percent of the marine protected areas are still exploited.

2   Coral reefs make better fishing areas than the open sea.

3   All of the coral reefs in the Philippines will be destroyed by 2050.

4   Humans are one reason why coral reefs are decreasing in size.

5   Available fish resources in the Philippines are expected to reduce by more than 50% over a period of seven years.

Remember: If you are answering a **YES, NO, NOT GIVEN** set of questions then you must complete the answer sheet with the words - **YES, NO** or **NOT GIVEN**. Do not write - **Y, N** or **NG** or - even worse - **TRUE, FALSE,** or **T** and **F**. As with every question type:

ALWAYS READ THE INSTRUCTIONS

11 - Headings

For many students this is the most difficult question type in the test and can waste a lot of time. Here you have to choose the most appropriate heading for each paragraph from a selection given to you. There are more headings in the list than you actually need.

Probably the best way to fully understand why each paragraph has been written is to read the whole paragraph but this takes time. Remember you have, on average, one and a half minutes per question and so quicker ways should be tried. There are several methods that are important to know about.

Method One

The main idea of a paragraph is expressed in the topic sentence and this is often the first sentence in a paragraph. Reading this could be enough to pick the correct heading.

Method Two

The last sentence of each paragraph provides a conclusion to the main idea in the paragraph and can lead to the correct heading.

Although, methods one and two can work very well they are not foolproof. Sometimes, these sentences can result in the wrong heading being picked. One reason this can happen is because there might be one or more sentences before the topic sentence, linking the new paragraph to the previous paragraph. If you only read the first sentence you might pick the heading for the previous paragraph.

In the same way the conclusion might be linking the existing paragraph to the next paragraph. This might end up with you choosing the heading for the next paragraph rather than the one you are reading.

However, if you have read the first and last sentences, but are still unsure, the third method might help.

Method Three

Information in the middle of the paragraph develops the main idea through an example, a definition, an analysis of the idea, a description of the point being discussed and so on. Through this you might understand more clearly (perhaps more easily than the topic sentence) what the main idea is and, therefore, what the heading should be.

How to pick a Heading

Example 1.

If the heading takes the form of a question then the paragraph must answer the question. If it doesn't, it cannot be the right heading. Look at the paragraph about the Northern Lights. The first sentence in the paragraph answers the heading question. The other sentences add further detail to the answer.

Heading : What causes the Northern Lights?

> <u>The Northern Lights are actually the result of collisions between gaseous particles in the Earth's atmosphere with charged particles released from the sun's atmosphere.</u> Variations in colour are due to the type of gas particles that are colliding. The most common auroral colour, a pale yellowish-green, is produced by oxygen molecules located about 60 miles above the earth. Rare, all-red auroras are produced by high-altitude oxygen, at heights of up to 200 miles. Nitrogen produces blue or purplish-red aurora.

Example 2.

The next heading is not a question but clearly states the paragraph must have information about problems concerning the asteroid theory. The first sentence introduces the main idea, the asteroid impact theory and problems associated with it. The other sentences develop the problems.

Heading : Problems with the Asteroid Theory

> Whilst an <u>asteroid</u> impact has gained ground over most other <u>theories</u>, there still remain <u>problems</u> with the theory. Palaeontologists have <u>yet to find</u> dinosaur fossils dating to the time of the impact, and <u>some evidence suggests</u> dinosaurs may have already been extinct before this event. In fact dinosaurs had been steadily declining for tens of thousands of years before the Chicxulub asteroid impacted.

Example 3.

You have seen in the first two examples (particularly example 2) that keywords can play an important part in pointing you towards the right heading. Keywords might, however, lead you to pick the wrong heading if you are not careful. Look at the next paragraph and decide which of the two headings provided is more suitable.

Heading 1 : Tea in China
Heading 2 : Tea in Japan.

> The exhibition also explores tea's enormous significance in **<u>Japan</u>**, where it was first introduced during the early Heian period (794-1185) by monks who travelled to <u>China</u> to study Zen Buddhism. Tea was consumed in monasteries and in some aristocratic circles, but it was not until the late 12th century that its role in art and culture became more prominent, after a Buddhist priest brought back to **<u>Japan</u>** the powdered tea (known as *matcha*) then popular in **<u>China</u>**.

In **Example 3**, the text mentions China twice, and Japan twice, with both sentences mentioning both countries. So, how do you decide which heading to choose? Read the paragraph again and decide which country is being stressed more.

Example 4.
The answer in the previous paragraph was Tea in Japan. Well done if you got it right. The next example shows two paragraphs - **A** and **B** - from an article about the formation of deserts around the world. Both paragraphs contain a few of the same words, **forest** / **forests** / **soil** / **soils** / **cultivation** / **problem** / **problems**

If a heading contains one or all of these words, it would be difficult to choose between the two paragraphs if you only base your judgment on these keywords. Remember, although keywords might be able to help you, it is also possible to have headings where words do not appear in the text.

Look at passages **A** and **B** and try to see what the main focus is in each paragraph and pick a suitable heading for each from the list above.

Heading 1 : Too much cultivation of forest soil
Heading 2 : Many problems but no solution
Heading 3 : A need to grow more food

A

The problem with this strategy is that more and more land gets used for cash crops, meaning that forests are destroyed to make way for more cultivation. Forest soils are often unsuitable for growing crops, and so turn into desert within a few years. Also, as more cash crops are grown, less land is used to grow crops to feed the people who live there. The balance needs to be changed so that less crops are grown for cash.

B

Soils can be ruined easily in areas where seasonal rainfall is unreliable. Cutting down forests and trees, over-cultivation of the soil and over-grazing can all contribute to desertification. In poorer countries, farmers often know what needs to be done, but they and their families live so near to starvation that they cannot even afford to buy what they need to keep their families healthy, let alone attempt to solve their problems.

The first paragraph here is focused more on crops (or cash crops) and the second paragraph focuses more on people (farmers and families). The most suitable headings would be the third heading for the first paragraph and the second heading for the second paragraph.

Remember:

This type of information can only be obtained quickly by developing your reading and scanning skills.

Example 5.
For the next three paragraphs (**A**, **B** and **C**) select the best heading from the three possible choices given above each paragraph. Do not focus only on keywords. Keywords will only help if they in some way reflect the main idea of the paragraph.

A.

Crossing the Channel Tunnel / Pullman Trains / Folkestone Harbour

The Pullman train terminates at Folkestone West (a small station just west of Folkestone Central), where passengers transfer to a waiting fleet of executive road coaches. Until 2007 the Venice Simplon Orient Express went down to Folkestone Harbour to meet the buses, reaching the Harbour station via a slow descent of the steep 1 in 30 gradient on the weed-strewn branch line to the seafront, a historic line once used by regular boat trains. The coaches cross the Channel somewhat unauthentically on board a vehicle-carrying shuttle train though the Channel Tunnel. At Calais, the coaches drive off the shuttle train at the Eurotunnel terminal and head for Calais Ville station. Calais Maritime station, where the ferries originally arrived to connect with the trains to Paris and beyond, was closed and tarmaced over in 1994 following the start of Eurostar services via the Channel Tunnel.

B.

Aboard the Titanic / Travelling in Style / Jaded Travellers

For four days the ship's elite passengers revelled in the brand new amenities of the Titanic, replete with every modern luxury known at the time. During the early part of the 20th century, it was considered quite sophisticated for wealthy families to spend portions of their time in Europe, which necessitated crossing the Atlantic at least once per year. Even to these jaded travellers, however, the Titanic ship was like no other. Nothing had been spared to ensure the comfort of the first class guests. The ship was even equipped with only 20 lifeboats, so that precious deck space for the first class passengers would not be taken up by bulky lifeboats.

C.

Beautiful Mansions and Statues / Heaven & Hell / Dharma and Sitagupta

The eastern half of the south gallery, the ceiling of which was restored in the 1930s, depicts the punishments and rewards of the 37 heavens and 32 hells. On the left the upper and middle tiers show fine gentlemen and ladies proceeding towards 18-armed Yama (the judge of the dead) seated on a bull; below him are his assistants, Dharma and Sitragupta. On the lower tier is the road to hell, along which the wicked are dragged by devils. To Yama's right, the tableau is divided into two parts by a horizontal line of Garuda (half-man, half-bird creatures): above, the elect dwell in beautiful mansions, served by women, children and attendants; below, the condemned suffer horrible tortures.

Heading Instructions

Each paragraph has been written with one main point to express. It is your job to find out what it is because this helps you pick the correct heading. One example is usually given and so you do not need to look at this paragraph. Start with the next paragraph that needs a heading. You can answer the questions in any order.

Questions 1 - 5

The reading passage has six paragraphs, A-F.

Choose the correct heading for paragraphs, B-F, from the list below.

	Headings
i	Bills of Exchange
ii	The English Civil War
iii	Gold standard
iv	The Knights Templar
v	Paper money
vi	Goldsmith bankers
vii	Chinese copper coins
viii	Virginian money
ix	Intangible money
x	The British pound

Example	Answer
Paragraph **A**	v

1 Paragraph **B**

2 Paragraph **C**

3 Paragraph **D**

4 Paragraph **E**

5 Paragraph **F**

Money

A In China the issue of paper money became common from about AD 960 onwards but there had been occasional issues long before that. A motive for one such early issue, in the reign of Emperor Hien Tsung 806-821, was a shortage of copper for making coins. A drain of currency from China, partly to buy off potential invaders from the north, led to greater reliance on paper money with the result that by 1020 the quantity issued was excessive, causing inflation. In subsequent centuries there were several episodes of hyperinflation and after about 1455, after well over 500 years of using paper money, China abandoned it.

B With the revival of banking in western Europe, stimulated by the Crusades, written instructions in the form of bills of exchange, came to be used as a means of transferring large sums of money and the Knights Templar and Hospitallers functioned as bankers. (It is possible that the Arabs may have used bills of exchange at a much earlier date, perhaps as early as the eighth century). The use of paper as currency came much later.

C During the English Civil War, 1642-1651, the goldsmiths' safes were secure places for the deposit of jewels, bullion and coins. Instructions to goldsmiths to pay money to another customer subsequently developed into the cheque (or check in American spelling). Similarly goldsmiths' receipts were used not only for withdrawing deposits but also as evidence of ability to pay and by about 1660 these had developed into the banknote.

D In England's American colonies a chronic shortage of official coins led to various substitutes being used as money, including, in Virginia, tobacco, leading to the development of paper money by a different route. Tobacco leaves have drawbacks as currency and consequently certificates attesting to the quality and quantity of tobacco deposited in public warehouses came to be used as money and in 1727 were made legal tender.

E Although paper money obviously had no intrinsic value its acceptability originally depended on its being backed by some commodity, normally precious metals. During the Napoleonic Wars convertibility of Bank of England notes was suspended and there was some inflation which, although quite mild compared to that which had occurred in other wars, was worrying to contemporary observers who were used to stable prices and, in accordance with the recommendations of an official enquiry, Britain adopted the gold standard for the pound in 1816.

F The break with precious metals helped to make money a more elusive entity. Another trend in the same direction was the growing interest in forms of electronic money from the 1990s onwards. In some ways e-money is a logical evolution from the wire transfers that came about with the widespread adoption of the telegraph in the 19th century but such transfers had relatively little impact on the everyday shopper.

Questions 1 - 5

The reading passage has six paragraphs, A-F.

Choose the correct heading for paragraphs, B-F, from the list below.

Headings
i   Symbols of emotion
ii   Blending therapies
iii   Isaac Newton
iv   The Middle Ages
v   Getting ready for war
vi   Freedom to choose
vii   Colours from nature
viii   Many positive uses
ix   Dying fabrics
x   Splitting colours

Example	Answer
Paragraph **A**	**vii**

1. Paragraph **B**
2. Paragraph **C**
3. Paragraph **D**
4. Paragraph **E**
5. Paragraph **F**

Colour Through the Ages

A The ancient Egyptians have been recorded to have been using colour for cures and ailments. They worshipped the sun, knowing that without light there can be no life. They looked at nature and copied it in many aspects of their lives. The floors of their temples were often green - as the grass which then grew alongside their river, the Nile. Blue was a very important colour to the Egyptians too; the colour of the sky. They built temples for healing and used gems (crystals) through which the sunlight shone. They would have different rooms for different colours. We could perhaps relate our present methods of colour/light therapy to this ancient practice.

B During the Middle Ages, Paracelsus reintroduced the knowledge and philosophy of colour using the power of the colour rays for healing along with music and herbs. Unfortunately, the poor man was hounded throughout Europe and ridiculed for his work. Most of his manuscripts were burnt, but now he is thought of, by many, to be one of the greatest doctors and healers of his time. A man, it would seem, very much ahead of his time. Not only do we now use colour therapy once again, but, his other ideas, using herbs and music in healing, can also be seen reflected in many of the complementary therapies now quite commonplace.

C A pioneer in the field of colour, Isaac Newton in 1672, published his first, controversial paper on colour, and forty years later, his work 'Opticks'. Newton passed a beam of sunlight through a prism. When the light came out of the prism it was not white but was of seven different colours: Red, Orange, Yellow, Green, Blue, Indigo and Violet. The spreading into rays was called dispersion by Newton and he called the different coloured rays the spectrum.

D Before World War II it was noted that a lot of red was being worn. Red in its most positive is the colour for courage, strength and pioneering spirit, all of which were much needed by the men and women who were fighting that war. However, in the most negative aspect, it is the colour of anger, violence and brutality. As the war was coming to an end, pale blue became a popular colour - an omen of the peace to come perhaps, also giving everyone the healing they must have so badly needed.

E We are lucky that we are now all able to choose any colour we like and can buy products of any colour freely. This was not always the case. In times gone by, the pigments used to dye fabrics violet/purple were very expensive and, therefore, only available to the wealthy. For example, the Romans in high office would wear purple robes since this, to them, indicated power, nobility and thus authority.

F We are now using colour in very positive ways again. Businesses are accepting that their employees may work better given a certain environment, and hospitals and prisons are also becoming aware of the effect that the colour around them can have on patients and prisoners respectively. Paint companies have introduced new colour cards with the therapeutic aspects of colour in mind. Cosmetic companies too have 'colour therapy' ranges included in their products. Colour has a great deal to offer us and can be found all around us in nature. We need to expand our awareness of colour so that we can truly benefit from nature's gifts so that 'colour' becomes a way of life, not just a therapy.

12 - Diagrams

The completion of a diagram question type involves finding the correct place in a passage and then labelling the diagram. The examples given here only show the paragraph with the relevant information in. You would need to find the right paragraph or paragraphs within the reading passage.

Simple Chemical Experiments

Hydrogen can be made very easily by using simple laboratory equipment. All you need is a thistle funnel, cork, glass dish, graduated glass cylinder, test tube, glass pipe, zinc, tap water, and hydrochloric acid. To begin with, 5ml of tap water is put into a 50ml graduated glass cylinder with about 1gm of zinc. The top of the glass cylinder is fitted with a cork and a thistle funnel and a glass pipe inserted into it. The glass pipe connects the cylinder with a glass dish. Sufficient tap water is placed in the dish to cover the top of the pipe which is then covered with a water filled test tube. Before adding 5 ml of hydrochloric acid to the funnel it is important to make sure that the end of the funnel is below the tap water. Once added, the hydrochloric acid comes into contact with the tap water very quickly and an immediate chemical reaction can be seen. Hydrogen gas is released and starts to travel down the pipe into the test tube. The hydrogen displaces the water and produces a test tube of pure hydrogen gas. By adding baking soda to the cylinder the acid solution is neutralized and can be poured down the sink.

Questions 1 - 8

The diagram below shows how hydrogen can be made using simple laboratory equipment.

Label the diagram.

Choose **NO MORE THAN THREE WORDS** *from the passage for each answer.*

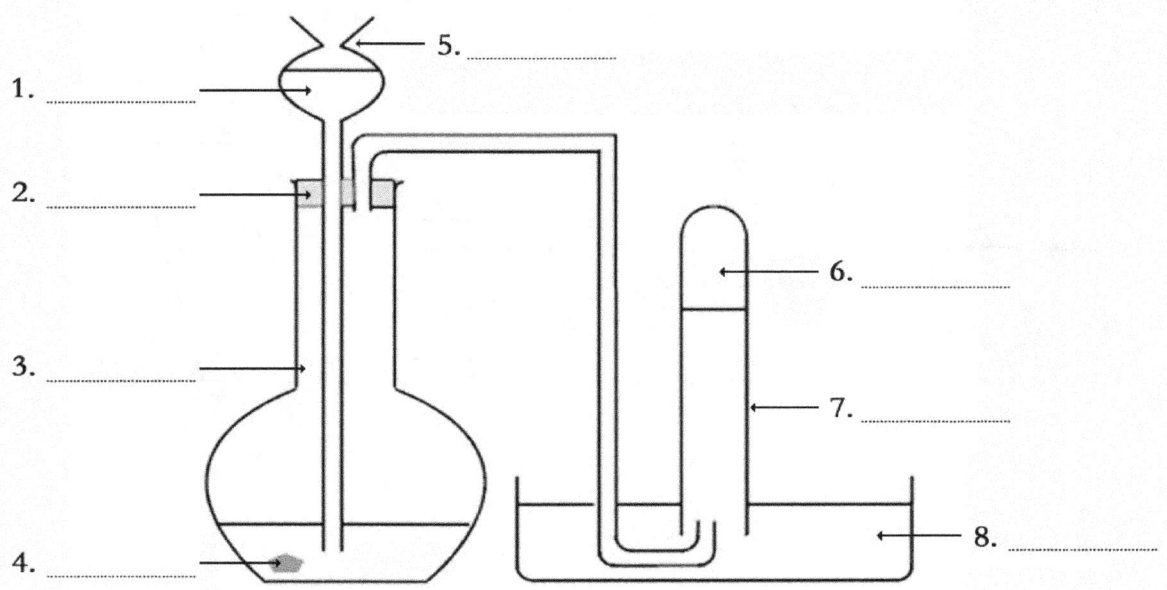

School Experiments

It is essential when conducting this experiment to wear safety goggles. This experiment is divided into four distinct sections. The first, the reaction stage, is when a glass beaker is placed on top of a tripod and 20cm of dilute sulphuric acid poured into it. The acid is then heated. When it is almost boiling, a small quantity of copper oxide powder is added to the beaker. The mixture is then stirred with a glass spatula until the copper oxide has dissolved. This process is then repeated until 1g of powder has been added to the sulphuric acid. The heat is then removed from the beaker and the solution allowed to cool. The second stage is the filtration stage and, as the name suggests, is where a filter and conical flask are used to remove any copper oxide that has not reacted. A clear copper sulphate solution will be left in the glass dish. The third stage is where heat is applied to the copper sulphate solution in order to concentrate the solution; the concentration stage. The final crystallization stage happens when the solution begins to cool and pure copper sulphate crystals start to form.

Questions 1 - 6

The diagram below shows how copper sulphate can be made using simple laboratory equipment.

Label the diagram.

*Choose **NO MORE THAN THREE WORDS AND/OR A NUMBER** from the passage for each answer.*

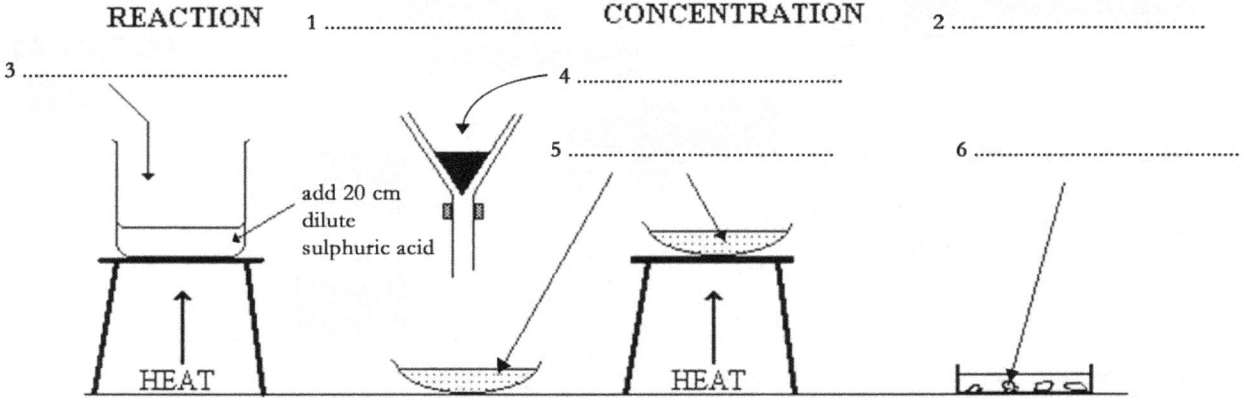

General Reading

Practice Tests 1 – 5

SECTION 1 *Questions 1-14*

Read the text below and answer Questions 1–6.

A

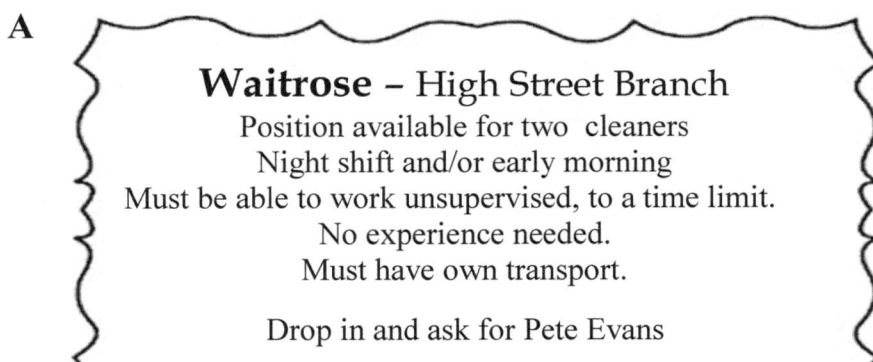

Waitrose – High Street Branch
Position available for two cleaners
Night shift and/or early morning
Must be able to work unsupervised, to a time limit.
No experience needed.
Must have own transport.

Drop in and ask for Pete Evans

B

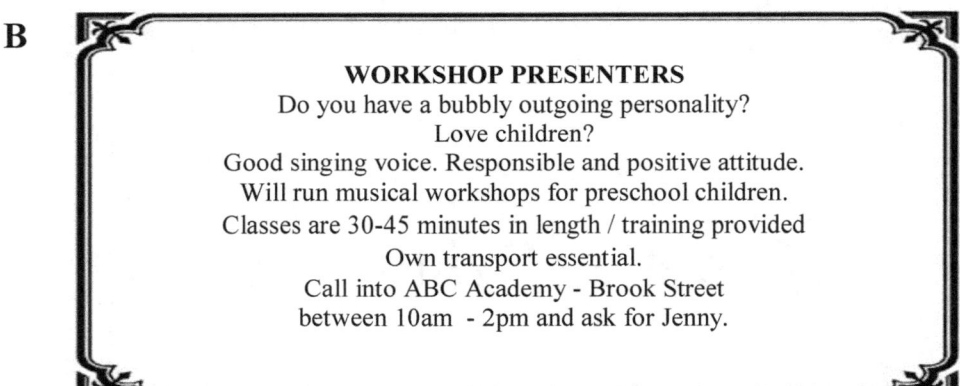

WORKSHOP PRESENTERS
Do you have a bubbly outgoing personality?
Love children?
Good singing voice. Responsible and positive attitude.
Will run musical workshops for preschool children.
Classes are 30-45 minutes in length / training provided
Own transport essential.
Call into ABC Academy - Brook Street
between 10am - 2pm and ask for Jenny.

C

Dog Walker
An animal loving person needed to walk our two lovely Yorkshire Terriers three times a week.
Evenings preferred.
No weekends
16 years or older is ideal
Call: 0916-202-7445 to apply

D

Nanny Wanted
To help look after two children - 2 and 5 years old.
Experience useful but patience and willingness to learn is enough.
Accommodation, food and pocket money provided.
Flexible working times.   Ideal for foreign student studying English.

Please send resume and photo to – Evelyn1978@hotmail.com

E

20 full time volunteers wanted
One year project.
Willing to relocate with free accommodation. Basic salary provided.
Supporting people with disabilities and young people from broken homes.
18-65 can apply.
Experience preferred but not essential.

F

Web-based company
Urgently requires a graphic designer
Working knowledge of Photoshop
College graduate preferred but enthusiastic computer nerd can apply.
Send short resume (with photo) to –

MegaBites, 10 Oak Road, Ashbourne

G

OLDE WORLDE CAFÉ
Waitress needed. (Full-time / Part-time)
Previous restaurant or café experience preferred.
Must be physically active and able to take orders.
Salary according to experience.
Will consider: high school graduate

Call 0245-67332 for interview. Ask for Mary.

TEST 1

Questions 1-6

*Look at the seven job advertisements, **A-G**, and read the descriptions of people below.*

Which is the most suitable job for each person?

*Write the correct letter, **A-G**, in boxes 1-6 on your answer sheet.*

1   a person willing to move location for one year. Salary is low but ideal for someone interested in social work

2   a high school student who loves exercise and animals with a few evenings free every week

3   an independent kind of person prepared to work at night or early mornings with transport

4   a high school graduate looking for their first job, must like talking to people

5   a cheerful person who loves working with young children who is able to sing and has own transport

6   a person who loves working with young children in return for a basic allowance, accommodation and time to study

Read the text below and answer Questions 7-14.

Mobile Phone Etiquette

Etiquette is a code of behavior that allows people to follow the standards accepted in society. Although these rules can change from country to county many similarities can be found. Many of the manners we develop are based on three categories; health, courtesy, and cultural norms. It is through these that we develop the customs and habits of a society.

Etiquette # 1
This is where you have to think more of others than yourself. Don't think of all those times that you had to put up with people talking on the phone in the cinema, on the train, and in the queue at McDonalds. Simply imagine all the ways other people will find you annoying if you use your mobile phone.

Etiquette # 2
The good thing about people is that sooner or later someone will tell you that you are annoying them. Their request to stop talking or talk quietly might seem unreasonable but if you really want to be a model mobile phone user just follow their request.

Etiquette # 3
To stop #2 from happening, and to keep your secrets to yourself then keep your distance - 3 metres - between you and anyone else.

Etiquette # 4
Even if you are following #3 you don't need to shout. This just makes it easier for people to hear you and much easier to annoy them.

Etiquette # 5
Remember, people don't want to hear you talking on the phone so they certainly don't want to hear the other person either. Don't turn your speaker on!

Etiquette # 6
If you don't want to be talked about keep your personal details to yourself. This means that #3 is probably not far enough from wagging ears. Either save the conversation for later or start using text messaging.

Etiquette # 7
Don't multi-task, it could cost you your life. Don't use the time you are spending in a queue to phone someone and certainly don't use the mobile phone when you are driving. In many countries this is illegal but it is also dangerous. National data show mobile phones were involved in 350 fatal crashes in 2011.

Etiquette # 8
There are many places such as a library, museum, theatre, and hospital where, hopefully, common sense tells you not use your phone.

TEST 1

Questions 7-14

Complete the notes below.

Choose **NO MORE THAN TWO WORDS AND/OR A NUMBER** *from the text for each answer.*

Write your answers in boxes 7-14 on your answer sheet.

NOTES ON MOBILE PHONE ETIQUETTE

Etiquette # 1
Don't think about the people you have met using their phone in front of or behind you.

Stop using your phone if you think people will find it **7** ....

Etiquette # 2
Other people will tell you about your phone etiquette. If they don't like it they might ask

you to **8** ....

Etiquette # 3
If you want to keep your **9** .... to yourself then keep **10** ....

Etiquette # 4
Even if you are not near anyone that is no excuse to shout. People will still hear you.

Etiquette # 5
Remember that people don't to hear you and so they definitely don't want to hear the

person you are talking to.

Etiquette # 6
If you really want to keep the conversation between the two of you then

11 .... is the best way to keep people from hearing.

Etiquette # 7
Trying to do too many things at once can be a problem. You know that using your mobile

in a **12** .... is frowned upon but using it in your car could be fatal. In America,

of all car accidents there were **13** ....fatalities in 2011 because the driver was

using a phone.

Etiquette # 8
Finally, if you have any **14** .... , you should know that talking on your mobile

in a theatre is a big no-no in mobile phone etiquette.

SECTION 2   Questions 15-27

Read the text below and answer Questions 15–21.

Savants

Super heroes like Superman have powers that are the envy of many children and even adults. Yet, we don't have to read comic books to find people with super powers. These

1. Leslie Lemke
Born blind, he was 15 when he eventually learnt how to walk. When he was 16 he played Tchaikovsky's Piano Concerto No. 1. after hearing this piece of music on the television the previous night. He is now able to play any piece of music simply by listening to it once.

2. Orlando Serrell
He was not born a savant. He was ten years old when he was hit on the head with a baseball. Since then he has been able to perform complicated calendar calculations and remember the weather every day from the day of the accident.

3. Kim Peek
Kim was the inspiration for the character played by Dustin Hoffman in the Rain Man. His nickname is "Kimputer" because he has read over 12,000 books and remembers everything about them. He reads two pages at once – his left eye reads the left page and his right eye reads the right page – in 3 seconds!

4. Stephen Wiltshire
When he was nine he learnt to talk but before this he had already developed a love for drawing. After a helicopter ride in Tokyo he drew an accurate and detailed view of the city on a piece of paper 10 metres long!

5. Ellen Boudreaux
Like Leslie Lemke, Ellen Boudreaux is a blind autistic savant with exceptional musical abilities. She can play music perfectly after hearing it just once. She can also walk around without bumping into things. She does this by making little chirping sounds that seem to act like a human sonar.

6. Daniel Tammet
Daniel is exceptionally gifted mathematically and linguistically. He can speak 11 languages fluently and learnt one of them, Icelandic, in 7 days. He appears normal but Daniel contends that he actually had to will himself to learn how to talk to and behave around people.

TEST 1

Questions 15-21

Look at the following statements and the list of savants below.

Match each statement with the correct savant, *A-F*.

Write the correct letter, *A-F*, in boxes 15-21 on your answer sheet.

NB You may use any letter more than once.

15   This savant reminds people of a computer as everything he reads he remembers.

16   This savant learnt one language very quickly and speaks many more.

17   This savant developed extraordinary powers after an accident.

18   This savant plays the piano.

19   This savant inspired a movie.

20   This savant avoids falling over with sonar like ability.

21   This savant loves to draw buildings with incredible accuracy.

	Savants
A	Leslie Lemke
B	Orlando Serrell
C	Kim Peek
D	Stephen Wiltshire
E	Ellen Boudreaux
F	Daniel Tammet

Read the text below and answer Questions 22-27.

Job Sharing

Job sharing is the perfect solution for people who want to carry on with their career but also raise a family. Before you do it you need to learn a few things as it can be more difficult than it might seem.

Job Sharing Is Like Marriage

When looking for a job share partner you need to look for someone that is the perfect teammate. You don't need to find someone who is a carbon copy of you but certainly they need to have a similar professional style, work ethic, and standards as you.

Job Sharing Relies on Communication

For a job share to work smoothly and efficiently you must work like one person. The transition from one person to another, from one day to the next must be seamless. Sharing information successfully can be done by setting up a shared email account, and using the same filing system to organise computer and paper files.

Be Flexible

No matter how well organized your schedule is things happen. Your child needs to visit the dentist. A friend flies in to visit you. A hundred and one reasons why you can't be at work tomorrow. If you have a good job sharing relationship then your partner will cover for you.

Job Sharing Means Less Income

This might be obvious but when you job share you not only share the work but you also share the income. That's right you will only get half the income maybe even less if you decide to do less than half the work.

You Share Accomplishments

Just as in a marriage many things you do, probably all the things you do, will be achieved because of you and your job share partner. In other words, you must share any praise for accomplishments.

Your Circumstances May Change

No matter how much you like your job, things change and so your commitment to it might also change. Things that you can't predict now might make you think about getting a fulltime job again; your spouse might move to another city, you decide to go back to university who knows what the future might bring?

TEST 1

Questions 22-27

Complete the sentences below.

*Choose **NO MORE THAN ONE WORD** from the passage for each answer.*

Write your answers in boxes 22-27 on your answer sheet.

22 You don't have to find an exact copy of you when looking for a job share partner but they must have similar ....

23 A successful job share means being able to share information with the same filing system so that each day flows into another in a .... manner.

24 One thing is certain and that is no matter how well prepared you are .... will happen.

25 An important thing to remember is that when you job share you won't get the .... of a fulltime job.

26 In a job share you can no longer accept all the ....

27 You might not always have the same .... because your life might be moving in another direction.

SECTION 3   Questions 28-40

Read the text below and answer questions 28-40.

Mission to Mars

2011 Mars One Founded
In 2011 Bas Lansdorp and Arno Wielders lay the foundation of the Mars One mission plan. Discussion meetings are held with potential suppliers of aerospace components in the USA, Canada, Italy and United Kingdom. Mission architecture, budgets and timelines are solidified from the feedback of supplier engineers and business developers. A baseline design for a mission of permanent human settlement on Mars achievable with existing technology is the result.

2013 Start Crew Selection
In April 2013, the Astronaut Selection Program is launched at press conferences in New York and Shanghai. Round One is an online application open to all nationalities. The selection program proceeds with three additional rounds over the course of two years. At the end of it around six teams of four individuals are selected for training. A new batch of the Astronaut Selection Program begins every year to replenish the training pool regularly. An analogue of the Mars habitat is constructed on Earth for technology testing and training purposes.

2015 Start of Crew Training
Selected candidates from the first batch of applicants enter full-time training groups. This training continues until the launch in 2024. The group's ability to deal with prolonged periods of time in a remote location is the most important part of their training. They learn to repair components of the habitat and rover, learn to grow their own food, and train in medical procedures. The first outpost simulation, a Mars-like terrain that is relatively easy to reach is chosen. A second training outpost is located at a more remote environment like the Arctic desert.

2018 Demo and Comsat Mission
A Demonstration Mission is launched to Mars in May 2018; it provides proof of concept for some of the technologies that are important for a human mission. A communication satellite is also launched that is placed into a Mars stationary orbit. It enables 24/7 communication between the two planets. It can relay images, videos and other data from the Mars surface.

2020 Rover Mission Launched
One intelligent rover and one trailer are launched. The rover can use the trailer to transport the landers to the outpost location. On Mars, the rover drives around the chosen region to find the best location for the settlement. An ideal location for the settlement is far enough north for the soil to contain enough water, equatorial enough for maximum solar power and flat enough to facilitate construction of the settlement. When the settlement location is determined, the rover prepares the surface for arrival of the cargo missions. It also clears large areas where solar panels will lie. A second communications satellite is launched into orbit around the Sun.

2022 Cargo Missions Launched
Six cargo missions are launched and two living units, two life support systems, and two supply units are sent to Mars in July 2022. In February 2023 all units land on Mars using a rover signal as a beacon.

2023 Outpost Operational
The six cargo units land on Mars, up to 10 km away from the outpost. The rover picks up the first life support unit using the trailer, takes it to the right place, and deploys the thin film solar panel of the life support unit. The rover can now connect to the life support unit to recharge its batteries much faster than using only its own panels, allowing it to do much more work. The rover picks up all the other cargo units and then deploys the thin film solar panel of the second life support unit and the inflatable sections of the living units. The life support unit is connected to the living units by a hose that can transport water, air and electricity.

The life support system is now activated. The rover feeds Martian soil into the life support system. Water is extracted from the Martian soil by evaporating the subsurface ice particles in an oven. The evaporated water is condensed back to its liquid state and stored. Part of the water is used for producing oxygen. Nitrogen and argon, filtered from the Martian atmosphere make up the other components of the breathable air inside the habitat.

2024 Departure Crew One
In April 2024, the components of the Mars transit vehicle are launched to Earth orbit on receiving the green light on the status of the systems on Mars. First, a transit habitat and a Mars lander with an assembly crew on-board are launched into an orbit around the Earth. The assembly crew docks the Mars lander to the transit habitat. Two propellant stages are launched a month later and are also connected. The first Mars crew, now fully trained, is launched into the same Earth orbit. In orbit the Mars One crew switches places with the assembly crew, who descend back to Earth. Engines of the propellant stages are fired and the transit vehicle is launched on a Mars transit trajectory. This is the point of no return; the crew is now bound to a 210-day flight to Mars.

Questions 28-31

Choose the correct letter, A, B, C or D.

Write the correct letter in boxes 28-31 on your answer sheet.

28 What is the plan to have a permanent human settlement on Mars based on?

    A new technology
    B new and old technology
    C existing technology
    D recent technology

29 How is the ideal site for the settlement found?

    A GPS
    B rover
    C the settlers
    D some luck

30 After the outpost is operational how does the rover recharge its batteries?

    A from the living units
    B from the life support unit
    C from its own solar panels
    D from the cargo units

31 Where does oxygen come from ?

    A Nitrogen and argon
    B water
    C Martian atmosphere
    D Life support system

TEST 1

Questions 32-38

Complete the summary below.

*Choose **NO MORE THAN TWO WORDS AND/OR NUMBER** from the passage for each answer.*

Write your answers in boxes 32-38 on your answer sheet.

To begin the process of selecting suitable astronauts two **32** _____ are held in two cities around the world. The first application is **33** _____ and available to every nationality. This is followed by a further **34** _____ rounds and results in the selection of **35** _____ teams that then start training. During training they learn how to cope with life in an isolated **36** _____ , cultivate **37**_____ , and perform **38** _____ .

Questions 39-40

Answer the questions below.

*Choose **NO MORE THAN TWO WORDS** from the passage for each answer.*

Write your answers in boxes 39-40 on your answer sheet.

39 How will it be possible for people on Mars to contact people on Earth?
40 What point is reached when the crew start their journey to Mars?

SECTION 1   Questions 1-14

Read the text below and answer Questions 1–6.

CORNWALL

A love affair that lasts a lifetime

It's hard not to fall in love with Cornwall. For some it's the happy memories of a childhood seaside holiday. For others it's the brief fling of a teenage summer. For most it's a passionate affair that lasts a lifetime…so let the affair begin!

Where is Cornwall?
Located in the far west of Great Britain, Cornwall is almost completely surrounded by the sea and has a magnificent 300 mile coastline. It is also the location of mainland Great Britain's most southerly promontory, The Lizard, and one of the UK's most westerly points, Land's End.

What's so special about it?
There are lots of things Cornwall is loved for; the dramatic coastline with its captivating fishing harbours; the spectacular beaches and the pounding surf that provide a natural playground for a variety of water sports; and of course the Cornish pasty and cream teas.

Expect the unexpected
But there are also lots of things about Cornwall that may surprise you. For instance, the wilderness of Bodmin Moor with its panorama of big skies. There's also the dynamic art scene found mainly in West Cornwall, inspired by the naturally stunning landscapes. More recently, Cornwall has become known for a food scene to rival London and beyond.

History and culture
Cornwall also has a tremendous history based on its Celtic roots; its Celtic Cornish culture; the warmth and friendliness of the people; and the Cornish language that can be seen in the village names. Cornwall is truly unique.

Why not visit some of Cornwall's most iconic experiences. From towering castles, beautiful gardens and places steeped in legends and history, you'll be spoilt for choice. Here are a few to get you started.

<u>Trebah Garden</u> - near Falmouth
One of the great gardens of Cornwall and rated among the 80 finest gardens in the world, discover the magic of this beautiful Cornish valley garden with over four miles of footpath.

<u>Lanhydrock</u> - Bodmin
Lanhydrock boasts a magnificent late Victorian country house with gardens and wooded estate. Discover two sides of Victorian life: those 'below stairs', and those 'upstairs'.

<u>Geevor Tin Mine</u> - near Penzance
Geevor tin mine is one of the largest preserved mine sites in the country and a Cornish Mining World Heritage Site. Housed in two acres of listed buildings, Geevor's collections and guides bring the story of Cornwall's rich industrial past to life.

TEST 2

Questions 1-6

Complete the sentences below.

Choose **NO MORE THAN THREE WORDS** from the passage for each answer.

Write your answers in boxes 1– 6 on your answer sheet.

1   Cornwall has stunning coastal views including the most ………………… point in Great Britain.

2   Apart from the coastal views, the amazing landscapes have inspired an unexpected but thriving ………………… .

3   Cornwall can now be compared to ………………… for its food and amazing chefs.

4   One thing that makes Cornwall different from the rest of England is its ………………… heritage.

5   The perfect place to discover insights into lifestyles from a bygone era is ………………… .

6   The perfect place to discover insights into Cornwall's industrial past is a ………………… .

Bees

Worker bees are between 8-19mm in length. They are divided into three distinct parts; head, thorax, abdomen. They have an almost completely black head, a thorax that is golden brown and black with patches of orange, and yellow bands can be easily seen on the abdomen. At the front of the head are two antennae for sensing their environment. They have four single wings. The largest are called forewings and the smallest hindwings. The hind legs are specialized for collecting pollen - each leg is flattened to form a pollen basket near the end of each leg.

Love them or hate them, we need bees to pollinate many important food crops, including most fruit and vegetables. Bee pollinated crops are important sources of vitamins A and C, and minerals like calcium. By pollinating attractive wildflowers like bluebells and poppies, bees also help support the natural environment that people love – benefitting us culturally and economically, as well as ecologically. Calculations from the University of Reading show that £510 million of annual total crop sales in the UK are pollinated by bees and other insects.

What would happen if there were suddenly no more bees to pollinate these crops? This is a question being asked by farmers, beekeepers, and scientists because bees are now dying in their millions and they want to know why.

It's widely recognised now that changes in agriculture are the main cause of bee decline across Europe. For example, hay meadows, which are full of many different plant species, have declined by 97 per cent since the 1930s, removing an important source of food for bees.

This has happened because of the trend towards growing the same crop (monocultures) over large fields. This has reduced the diversity of flowers available and resulted in the removal of hedges. Species that have more specialised food needs, like the Shrill Carder Bee, have been particularly hard hit. It is now listed as an endangered species.

With less hedges bees find it more difficult to move between feeding and nesting sites. This is because hedges act as corridors for bees to move along, but with less hedges movement becomes more difficult.

Pests and diseases are also a major threat to honey bees and other managed bees. The Varroa mite is thought to be one of the main causes of native honey bee loss. The impact on wild bees is harder to assess but 'spill-over' of diseases and pests between wild and managed bees has increasingly been observed.

Climate change has an affect as it can alter the timing of plant flowering, or the time that bees come out of hibernation, which means bees may emerge before there is enough food available.

TEST 2

Questions 7-10

*Choose the correct letter, **A**, **B**, **C** or **D**.*

Write the correct letter in boxes 7-10 on your answer sheet.

7   Apart from pollinating crops how else do bees help us?

    A   economically
    B   culturally
    C   ecologically
    D   all of the above

8   Why have the variety of flowers available for bees to pollinate fallen ?

    A   conservation measures
    B   less hedges
    C   fertilizers
    D   urban development

9   There are many reasons for the decline in bees but what is one of the major reasons for shrinking numbers of native honey bees?

    A   Varroa mites
    B   spill-over
    C   managed bees
    D   hard to assess

10   Why might bees end their hibernation at a different time?

    A   to pollinate more flowers
    B   to get more food
    C   climate change
    D   to emerge with other bees

Questions 11-14

The diagram below shows the worker bee.

Label the diagram.

*Choose **NO MORE THAN TWO WORDS** from the passage for each answer.*

Write your answers in boxes 11-14 on your answer sheet.

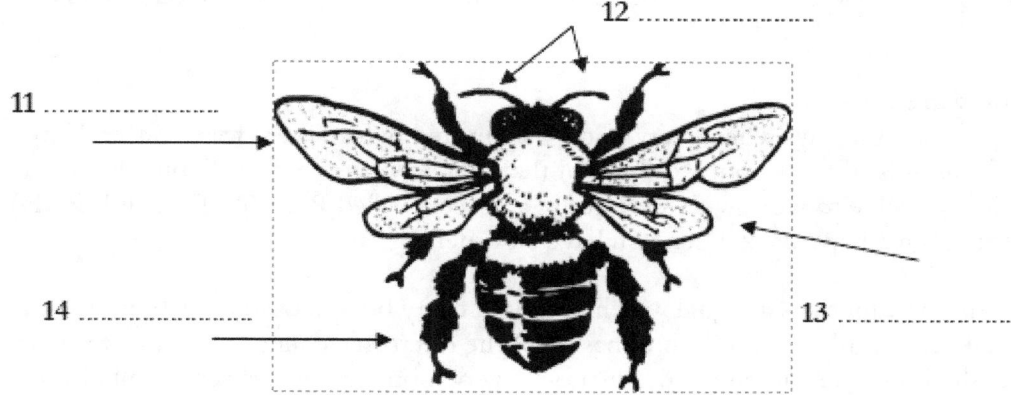

TEST 2

SECTION 2 Questions 15-27

Read the text below and answer Questions 15–20.

The Printing Process

The world entered its first information revolution when the first printing press was built in 1450. Before this, typical ways of recording information were to carve words onto clay tiles and bamboo, or to write on parchment or papyrus. Fast forward to the digital age, the second information revolution, and it has now become possible to self-publish, have books printed in paperback or as an e-book, and some books are even free!

Digital warehouse

Long gone are the days when every book was printed before there was a buyer. Why print thousands of books only to find out that very few people want to buy them? Now it is possible to work with a printer in a process called Print On Demand (POD) and only print a paperback when you have an order.

To do this a printer has a digital warehouse with every book stored electronically. Once an order is placed, the printer has all of the electronic data necessary to print and deliver the book to its intended destination. Every month money is sent to all of the authors that have sold books that month.

Giving your book to the printer

Once written, an author can send his book electronically to the printer in the form of a PDF file or as a hardcopy that can be scanned and digitized by the printer. Processing fees for all services from a printer are minimal but allow you to have access to large distribution networks of not only online bookstores but also the bricks and mortar retailers. These people may not buy your book but your book will be in their catalogues and they will order from the printer if someone asks for it.

Two Concerns

Speed is not the only priority for the printer, they are also concerned with quality and have 10 quality control checks on each book before it is shipped.

Sharp graphics and crisp text make it virtually impossible to distinguish a POD book from the more traditional offset copies. As technology continues to improve this can only get better.

As an author, it is possible to choose the type of book you want; paperback, hardback, or e-book (now the most popular form of book), the size of your book, type of paper, and type of cover (laminated, cloth or jacketed for hardbacks).

Questions 15-20

Complete the sentences below.

*Choose **NO MORE THAN THREE WORDS** from the passage for each answer.*

Write your answers in boxes 15–20 on your answer sheet.

15 We experienced our first information revolution with the development of the ....

16 It is no longer necessary to print books in their ....

17 Print On Demand works by making sure that the printer has been given all of the relevant ....

18 If necessary the printer will scan and digitize your ....

19 Latest technology makes the difference between offset printing and Print On Demand almost .... to tell.

20 Apart from the traditional hardback and paperback books authors can now publish in .... form.

TEST 2

Read the text below and answer Questions 21–27.

Yoga

Developed more than 5,000 years ago, yoga can be a way of life that benefits you physically, mentally, and spiritually. But where to start? Here is a quick summary of five of the most common yoga styles practiced today.

Hatha	
	Originated in India in the 15th century. Slow-paced, gentle, and focuses on breathing and meditation.
Purpose	Introduces beginners to yoga with basic poses and relaxation techniques.
Benefits	Relieves stress, provides physical exercise, and improves breathing.
Good for	Beginners wanting to learn the basics of yoga.
Vinyasa	
	Similar to Hatha, basic poses and breath-synchronized movements. Stresses the Sun Salutation, 12 poses where movement is matched to the breath.
Purpose	Links the breath with movement, builds lean muscle mass throughout the body.
Benefits	Helps improve strength and flexibility, tones the abdominal muscles, and reduces the risk of heart disease, high blood pressure, and type 2 diabetes.
Good for	Beginners and advanced yogis alike seeking to strengthen their bodies.
Ashtanga	
	Metaphorically focuses on **eight limbs**. Fast-paced, intense with lunges, push-ups.
Purpose	Helps improve one's spiritual self.
Benefits	Relieves stress, improves coordination, and helps with weight loss.
Good for	Fit people looking to maintain strength, stamina, and spirituality.
Iyengar	
	Covers all eight aspects of Ashtanga yoga and focuses on bodily alignment. Standing poses are emphasized, and are often held for long periods of time.
Purpose	Strengthens and brings the body into alignment.
Benefits	Helps improve balance, speeds up recovery from injury, builds up body strength.
Good for	Beginners who want to learn the correct alignments in each pose and those with injuries, balance issues, and chronic medical conditions like arthritis.
Bikram	
	Practiced in a 95 to 100 degree room. A series of 26 poses that allows for a loosening of tight muscles and sweating.
Purpose	Flushes out toxins and deeply stretches the muscles.
Benefits	Speeds up recovery from an injury, enhances flexibility, and cleanses the body.
Good for	Beginners, advanced yogis who want to push themselves and those with injuries.

Questions 21-27

Look at the following statements and the list of yoga styles below.

*Match each statement with the correct style, **A-E**.*

*Write the correct letter, **A-E**, in boxes 21-27 on your answer sheet.*

***NB** You may use any letter more than once.*

21 A style where breathing and movement are in harmony.
22 A style that focuses on improving your posture.
23 A style for starters wanting to improve their breathing.
24 A style that can help recovery from an injury and helps with posture.
25 A style for someone hoping to lose weight.
26 A style that helps muscles relax.
27 A style that helps you to develop your spirituality.

	Yoga Styles
A	Hatha
B	Vinyasa
C	Ashtanga
D	Iyengar
E	Bikram

TEST 2

SECTION 3 Questions 28-40

Read the text below and answer Questions 28–40.

British Study Centres
English Language School

English for Life
Language courses at British Study Centres are planned and delivered to equip students with the language skills they need to achieve their future dreams. This is achieved through ongoing structured dialogue between the student and teacher involving the use of tutorials, needs analysis questionnaires and so on.

School Locations
Study English in four of the UK's most exciting cities: London, Oxford, Brighton and Bournemouth.

English Courses
Choose from a range of General English, Exam Preparation (including IELTS) and Business English programmes.

History of British Study Centres
British Study Centres was founded in the 1930s by Joseph Cleaver, grandfather of current Chairman and Chief Executive, Simon Cleaver.

The state-of-the-art Oxford language school is fitted with the very best in language learning facilities, offering students a unique modern learning experience. To this day the Company remains a family firm privately owned and managed by Simon and his family.

In the early days the Company concentrated on correspondence courses and quickly established offices and examination centres across the entire (then) British Empire and beyond and in the process became the UK's largest group of correspondence colleges.

In the 1970s, the Company, now run by Joseph's sons, James and Thomas, began to focus on face-to-face tuition with the establishment of vocational colleges in London, Oxford and Brighton.

In the 1990s the Company established its first English language school in Oxford in 1996 followed by Brighton in 2002 and London in 2004. Since then all of these schools have expanded to cope with increasing demand.

In 2008 the Company moved into the young learners market with the acquisition of ICH (International College Holidays) that specialized in vacation courses for 10-15 years olds. They now run these courses in 5 institutes including the University of Brighton.

In 2010 the fourth school for adults opened in the south coast town of Bournemouth. In the same year they opened a specialist Teacher Training Facility in Oxford.

In 2012 live online lessons were launched with teachers using the latest video conferencing technology.

In recent years the Company has been honoured to win a number of awards associated with the language school industry, including twice winner of Study Travel Magazine's coveted 'Star' English Language School Europe award in 2010 and 2012, and winner of Study Travel Magazine's 'Star' Junior Courses for under 18s in 2012.

Study English in Oxford BSC, a City Made for Students!

40,000 students and 39 unique university colleges give Oxford a very special 'student' atmosphere – an ideal place to learn English! It has a deserved worldwide reputation for the quality of education. Oxford University is the oldest English speaking university in the world, dating back to 1249. It is consistently ranked in the top three in the world. Oxford is located in the heart of England and benefits from excellent road and rail links to London (50 minutes) and the rest of the UK. The city sits on the banks of the Thames and boasts a variety of world-famous museums, galleries and libraries. Besides the traditional, there are hundreds of modern restaurants, pubs, clubs and riverside cafes to enjoy.

Key Facts for Oxford BSC	
No. of students (peak season)	325
No. of students (low season)	175
Average age	25
Minimum age	16
Average class size	11 (max 14)

TEST 2

Questions 28-34

Complete the table below.

Choose **NO MORE THAN THREE WORDS AND/OR A NUMBER** from the passage for each answer.

Write your answers in boxes 28-34 on your answer sheet.

Year	Events in British Study Centres
1930s	First established by current owner's grandfather **28** _____
1970s	Three **29** _____ were opened as the new face of the Company.
1990s	The first English language school was opened in Oxford.
30 _____	Six years after the first school another was opened in Brighton.
31 _____	The third school was then opened in **32** _____ .
2008	The University of Brighton is now one of **33** _____ where vacation courses are held for youngsters.
2010	Another school was opened.
2012	**34** _____ made it possible to have lessons online.

Questions 35-40

Do the following statements agree with the information given in the reading passage?

In boxes 35-40 on your answer sheet, write

    YES   *if the statement reflects the claims of the writer*
    NO   *if the statement contradicts the claims of the writer*
    NOT GIVEN   *if it is impossible to say what the writer thinks about this*

35 There is not much interaction between the student and teacher.

36 James Cleaver is Simon Cleaver's father.

37 Oxford University is the oldest university in the world.

38 There are a few banks by the Thames.

39 They never teach students older than 25.

40 They never have more than 14 students in the class.

TEST 3

SECTION 1 Questions 1-14

Read the text below and answer Questions 1–6.

Gourmet Restaurants

Gordon Ramsey – Claridge's, London		
Average Score:		The waiters were excellent. Table always kept clean, water glasses topped up, warm bread basket refilled. Even invited to see the kitchen. Everything was faultless. The slow cooked lamb was one of the best main courses I have ever had. Finished with coffee and chocolates.
Quality of Service	5	
Quality of Food	5	
Value for Money	5	

David Tang - China Tang – The Dorchester, London		
Average Score:		I have had better for a quarter of the price. We told the manager that we were celebrating my husband's birthday but they did nothing special for us. However, a table close to us were celebrating a birthday and got special treatment.
Quality of Service	3	
Quality of Food	1	
Value for Money	1	

Rick Stein – The Seafood Restaurant, Padstow		
Average Score:		Went after talking to friends who had been. Not an impressive location as they have a pay and display car park in front of it. Excellent from start to finish. Rick Stein has been a big inspiration to me. We were on a two-week holiday and visited two other Master Chef restaurants including Jamie Oliver's Fifteen but this was the best by far.
Quality of Service	3.5	
Quality of Food	3.5	
Value for Money	2.5	

Jamie Oliver – Fifteen, London		
Average Score:		The service is rather poor. We were a large party of 12 celebrating my birthday and this added to an already overwhelmed staff. Food absolutely appalling and would have been better if they had used a microwave. Food was either salty or bland.
Quality of Service	4.5	
Quality of Food	3.5	
Value for Money	3.5	

Gordon Ramsey – Maze, London		
Average Score:		Two free glasses of champagne on entering the restaurant. Very relaxed atmosphere. Friendly staff. Met Gordon at our table. The kitchen is spotless. The service was slow but wonderful food.
Quality of Service	4	
Quality of Food	5	
Value for Money	4.5	

Questions 1-6

Look at the following statements and the list of gourmet restaurants below.

*Match each statement with the correct restaurant, **A-E**.*

*Write the correct letter, **A-E**, in boxes 1-6 on your answer sheet.*

***NB** You may use any letter more than once.*

1. Excellent food but not a good view from the restaurant.
2. Spoilt a birthday celebration and food was far too expensive.
3. Complimentary drinks and wonderful food.
4. Inspired by the owner and encouraged to go by word-of-mouth.
5. The waiters were very attentive.
6. Spoilt a birthday celebration and food was terrible.

Gourmet Restaurants
A Claridge's
B China Tang
C The Seafood Restaurant
D Fifteen
E Maze

Read the text below and answer Questions 7-14.

GREGGS Bakery

Greggs plc is the largest bakery chain in the United Kingdom and has 1,671 outlets. It specialises in savoury products such as pasties, sausage rolls but also sells sandwiches and sweet items including doughnuts and vanilla slices.

The Perfect Start to your Day
Why not get your day off to a great start with the perfect meal? Treating yourself to a tasty breakfast instantly brightens up a morning, making that long day at the office seem much more bearable.

Café and Shop prices are different. Why?
Firstly, VAT is applicable for a 'sit down service'. In addition, our running costs are greatly increased in terms of additional team members, cutlery, tables, extra cleaning required, and so on, which unfortunately means it is more expensive to run a café operation.

Which of your products are suitable for vegetarians?
We have a range of sandwiches and savouries which are meat free including Egg Mayonnaise, Cheese Savoury and Cheese and Tomato. We also have the Cheese & Onion Pasty and Cheese & Tomato Pizza, which are made solely with vegetarian ingredients and don't contain any animal derivatives or animal rennet.

Do you have allergy free products?
Unfortunately, we're unable to recommend any of our products to people with allergies because our food is freshly baked and prepared in open bakery and shop environments so cross-contamination could inadvertently occur.

Why is mayo on so many sandwiches?
We have introduced 'no mayo' sandwiches which are clearly labelled. In addition, if we have the ingredients and you'd really like your sandwich without mayonnaise, we will try and do this for you. Just ask at the counter.

What kind of Greggs gifts can I buy?
We offer three different kinds of gifting options; a Gift Card, an e-Gift, and an m-Gift.

Gift Card
Give a Greggs Gift Card to someone and they can buy anything they like from Greggs. It's the perfect way to say thanks - to wish them a happy birthday - or just as a surprise to show that you care.

e-gift
Send the gift of Greggs by email. It's simple, secure and won't cost you a penny in postage. You can pick the email design, add a personal message and choose exactly when it's delivered.

m-gift
Want to send a Greggs Gift Card to their mobile phone? Choose an m-gift and we'll text it to their mobile phone so they can shop at Greggs straight away.

Questions 7-14

Do the following statements agree with the information given in the reading passage?

In boxes 7-14 on your answer sheet, write

TRUE *if the statement agrees with the information*
FALSE *if the statement contradicts the information*
NOT GIVEN *if there is no information on this*

7   They have the largest bakery shops in the United Kingdom.

8   They only sell pasties, sausage rolls, in their savoury product range.

9   Lots of people complain because the cafe prices are more than the shop prices.

10   Vegetarians can't eat doughnuts as they have animal derivatives or rennet in them.

11   Food could cause an allergic reaction because they like to mix baked food together.

12   They can always prepare made-to-order sandwiches by asking at the counter.

13   Greggs pay for the postage when delivering e-gifts.

14   If you have forgotten to bring some money you could pay by mobile phone.

SECTION 2   Questions 15-27

Read the text below and answer Questions 15 – 21.

The London Pass

Established in 1999, The London Pass is a sightseeing city card that helps visitors make the most of their trip to London, saving them both time and money.

The London Pass Saves You Money
London can be an expensive city, and its tourist attractions are no exception. However, go sightseeing with a London Pass and you could make some great savings – not to mention saving the hassle of queuing to buy entry tickets and carrying around change.

The London Pass Saves You Time
London is a popular destination; therefore, attractions and sights do get very busy. Waiting in line can sometimes take hours from your sightseeing experience - that's why London Pass holders get to skip the queue at key attractions such as Tower of London, Windsor Castle and the London Bridge Experience. Get VIP treatment and go straight to the front with your London Pass.

The London Pass Saves You Stress
Carrying lots of cash around and having to figure out how much an attraction will cost can take the fun out of your sightseeing adventure. Your London Pass is the ticket into every attraction – so you don't need to worry about buying separate admissions or working out how much it costs, it's all done for you in one simple pass.

With every London Pass you get the following:

- **Free entry to over 60 attractions**, tours, sights and museums
- **Fast Track Entry** - ability to skip the lines at various selected attractions to save time
- **Optional Travelcard** to cover all of your transport needs
- **A useful 160+ page guidebook** (one per Adult London Pass) about the attractions plus helpful tips about the city
- Over 20 exclusive special offers
- Money Back Guarantee option available

London Pass Attraction	Normal Adult Entry Price
Tower of London	£19.50
Thames River Cruise	£17.00
London Bridge Experience	£24.00
Windsor Castle	£17.75
London Zoo	£22.80

Questions 15-21

Complete the sentences below.

*Choose **NO MORE THAN THREE WORDS AND/OR A NUMBER** from the passage for each answer.*

Write your answers in boxes 15-21 on your answer sheet.

15 The London Pass is the best way to save time and money when ....

16 You save time because there is no longer a need to ....

17 You won't have to calculate how much money you have left because the London Pass is ....

18 If you are planning to see as much of London as possible you could consider a ....

19 If you are not happy with the various attractions and special offers we provide you can take advantage of our ....

20 If a leisurely few hours on a boat sounds good then try our ....

21 You save exactly .... when you visit the London Bridge Experience.

TEST 3

Read the text below and answer Questions 22–27.

The Body Shop

The Body Shop International PLC, known as **The Body Shop**, has a range consisting of 1,200 products, including cosmetics and make-up in its 2,500 franchised stores in 61 countries.

The company, which has its international headquarters in Littlehampton, West Sussex, England, was founded in 1976 by Anita Roddick and is now part owned by parent company L'Oréal corporate group.

In 1970 Anita visited "The Body Shop" in California. It was part of a car repair shop and they sold naturally-scented soaps and lotions. In 1976, Anita opened a similar shop in the UK, using the same business name.

From its first launch in the UK in 1976, The Body Shop experienced rapid growth, expanding at a rate of 50 percent annually.

The opening of Roddick's first modest shop received early attention when the Brighton newspaper, The Evening Argus, carried an article about an undertaker with a nearby store who complained about the use of the name "The Body Shop."

In March 2006, The Body Shop agreed to a £652.3 million takeover by L'Oréal. It was reported that Anita and Gordon Roddick, who set up The Body Shop 30 years previously, made £130 million from the sale.

The Body Shop turned increasingly toward social and environmental campaigns to promote its business in the late 1980s. In 1997, Roddick launched a global campaign to raise self-esteem in women and against the media stereotyping of women. It focused on unreasonably skinny models in the context of rising numbers suffering from bulimia and anorexia.

Following her death in 2007, Prime Minister Gordon Brown paid tribute to Dame Anita, calling her "one of the country's true pioneers" and an "inspiration" to businesswomen. He said: "She campaigned for green issues for many years before it became fashionable to do so and inspired millions to the cause by bringing sustainable products to a mass market. She will be remembered not only as a great campaigner but also as a great entrepreneur."

In October 2009, The Body Shop was awarded a 'Lifetime Achievement Award' by the RSPCA in Britain, in recognition of its uncompromised policy which ensures ingredients are not tested on animals by its suppliers.

TEST 3

Questions 22-27

Choose the correct letter, A, B, or C.

Write the correct letter in boxes 22-27 on your answer sheet.

22 Who owns the company now?

   A Anita Roddick and her parents.
   B Body Shop and L'Oréal.
   C L'Oréal.

23 How did Anita Roddick decide on the name "The Body Shop"?

   A The name came to her in a dream.
   B She copied the name from an undertaker.
   C She took the name from a store in America.

24 What happened three decades after launching "The Body Shop"?

   A They retired.
   B They bought L'Oréal.
   C They accepted a takeover bid by L'Oréal.

25 How did "The Body Shop" promote itself?

   A by stereotyping women
   B socially
   C through environmental and social issues

26 What did Anita do about very skinny models?

   A She gave them some food.
   B She tried to empower women around the world.
   C They started to work for her.

27 What did Gordon Brown say about Anita Roddick?

   A She was a pioneer for environmental issues.
   B She was very fashionable.
   C She made the mass market sustainable.

TEST 3

SECTION 3   Questions 28-40

Read the text below and answer Questions 28 – 40.

Ecotourism

Ecotourism Guidelines for Travelers

There is a well known motto for all ecotourists:

"Take only photographs, leave only footprints."

This is really the essence of being a tourist in an eco tour, but to be that perfect needs time. To make sure you get the most out of your holiday before, during and after your trip, and show the respect the people and places you go to deserve, follow the guidelines shown here.

A

Educate yourself as much as possible about your destination. It can be useful to learn a little about not only current events but also the culture, customs and history of the area. Spend a little time learning some of their language even if it's only hello, please, thank you and numbers. People will appreciate the effort you have made to communicate with them. What can you find out about their ecosystems? What animals are endangered and why?

B

One reason to find out something about where you are going and the people who live there is so that you don't start offending them as soon as you step off the plane. The old saying, "When in Rome do as the Romans do" can be quite useful when thinking about what to wear. Not everyone dresses the same and some people might be more conservative than you are. Do not judge the people or their cultural habits by using your own cultural values. The differences between you are just that – differences – and are not a sign of one culture being wrong or inferior.

C

While we might think nothing of hanging a Nikon around our neck or walking around with an iPad, in many places these are seen as signs of very rich people. In brief, be sensitive to cultural status symbols as these can create barriers between you and the local people. And remember, that ring in the nose that you are laughing at might just mean you are making fun of the local chief!

D

It's very common for tourists to want to give little gifts of friendship to people they meet. Stop and think like an ecotourist. How many little children have greeted you on your travels by holding out their hand and asking for money? Maybe they started to beg when they realised that tourists have more money than they do and have sweets or pencils in their bag. It is far better to donate money or supplies to a local organisation that can be found either by research or asking your tour operator.

E
Expect the unexpected as eco holidays can be far more unpredictable than a package holiday but can provide experiences of a lifetime. Take changes to your plans as an opportunity to learn and a chance to become closer to the culture that you are now living in. This is the time to be flexible and adapt to the situation.

F
A large luxury hotel in the middle of nowhere takes far more resources to build and maintain than does a small family run inn. So, expect to stay in more basic settings; maybe very basic. This is part of the learning experience and will help bring you closer to understanding the lives of the people who actually live there. Resources might be a problem and so the influx of tourists will only add to the problems. Be sensitive to this especially when washing becomes a luxury and food is as far removed from fine dining as it can be.

G
What you do when you are there can affect the lives of the people who live there after you have left. With this in mind use makeshift bathrooms at least 70 metres from any water source. Take all trash with you and if you find things left by other tourists then take that too. Don't take any souvenirs back with you especially if you have bought parts of endangerd animals like feathers, claws and skin. You are only helping to create a little business and the demise of another animal species.

H
Always consider how your visit can benefit the local economy. Are you adding to their problems or in some way helping them? This is an integral part of true ecotourism. Think local and start to use local transportation, guides, inns, restaurants and markets. This helps create an economy that is based on positive alternatives to potentially destructive practices and can involve the whole community. This is the true essence of ecotourism.

I
A true ecotourist is also an ambassador for his or her country. If we are honest, the image of western travellers is not always a good one but you can change this. Take the opportunity to talk to local people in a real exchange of cultural experiences. Never miss an opportunity to get to know someone; it could be the person sitting next to you on a local bus, or the person cooking your dinner. Take the chance when you can.

J
Once home, your journey should continue. Share your experiences with anyone who will listen. Try to send money to one of the local organizations or write an article for one of the papers in your town. As much as possible try to promote the place you have been to and encourage other people to go to experience what you have.

TEST 3

Questions 28-32

The text has ten paragraphs, *A-J*.

Which paragraph contains the following information?

Write the correct letter, **A-J**, in boxes 28-32 on your answer sheet.

28   be prepared to live simply
29   be a role model by mixing with the locals
30   respect cultural differences
31   your adventure never stops
32   be careful about how you show your friendship

Questions 33-37

Complete the summary below.

Choose **NO MORE THAN FOUR WORDS** from the passage for each answer.

Write your answers in boxes 33– 37 on your answer sheet.

It is important to remember that a Nikon camera in one culture might be like a

33 _____ for another in terms of social position. Giving a small gift as a token of your

34 _____ might encourage some children 35 _____ . Being an ecotourist guarantees

that your holidays won't be like 36 _____ . So relax and learn to 37 _____ .

Questions 38-40

Answer the questions below.

Choose **NO MORE THAN THREE WORDS** from the passage for each answer.

Write your answers in boxes 38– 40 on your answer sheet.

38   What are you recommended to do before you start your travels?
39   What might other tourists leave behind?
40   What should a positive local economy try to avoid?

SECTION 1   Questions 1-14

Read the text below and answer Questions 1– 6.

How to Book a Course

If you are interested in joining any of our adult evening classes you can now book in a number of different ways.

Online
Search for course information online and enrol using our online form. Please upload a passport size photo and pay using any major credit card or PayPal.

In person
Call into the Adult Education Centre bringing with you:
- your enrolment form
- the correct fee (you can make payment by credit/debit card, cheque or cash)
- passport size photo

By post
Print out the enrolment form provided online. Make cheques payable to Cornwall Council.
Please enclose:
- your enrolment form
- the correct tuition fee
- passport size photo

and send to: Cornwall Council, Adult Education Centre, Room 308, Sedgemoor Centre, Priory Road, St Austell, PL25 5AB

Forms are also available at your local library

By phone
Ring our enquiry line number: **0898 - 275395**
Please have your credit or debit card details ready:
- name of card holder
- card number (inc. last 3 digits on signature strip)
- expiry date

If the phone is engaged please keep trying or leave a message for us to call you back.

Remember to book your course at least one week before the start date.

Course fees
The course fees are printed with the course details and are exempt from VAT.

Refunds
A full refund of course fees will only be made if a class does not start or closes due to insufficient enrolments. Refunds for other reasons are not generally given, but if a refund is granted there will be an administration charge of £5.00.

Flexible Learning Centres
Adult Education Centres can be found in six towns in Cornwall. Call in to your local Centre or phone for details of opening times and courses available.

TEST 4

Questions 1-6

Complete the sentences below.

Choose NO MORE THAN THREE WORDS AND/OR A NUMBER *from the passage for each answer.*

Write your answers in boxes 1-6 on your answer sheet.

1 If you decide to book in person don't forget to bring your photo, form, and ………………… .

2 If you decide to pay by post you can find the ………………… online.

3 If you are having problems booking over the phone we can ………………… .

4 Regardless of how you book do it a minimum of ………………… before.

5 All of are courses are free from …………………

6 ………………… is the only reason we would provide a full refund.

Read the text below and answer Questions 7-14.

Holiday Cottages

Glen Cottage	
Accommodation	up to 2 people
Family	no children
Parking	2 cars
Distance to the sea	3 miles
Reviews: Lots of amazing walks. Fantastic scenery and lovely garden. The property was perfect. There is nothing I would have changed. There is ample parking in the driveway. The owners, who live in the thatched cottage nearby, are very friendly and permit the use of their beautiful landscaped garden. This has some fabulous ponds, shrubs and plants, and guests have the use of a private summerhouse.	

Tregonning	
Accommodation	up to 3 people
Family	no under 2's
Parking	1 car
Distance to the sea	Less than 1 mile
Reviews: Thank you for the welcome tray and the flowers. The best priced accommodation we have ever stayed in. One week is too short! It really is a home from home with everything we could possibly need provided. By far the best equipped, central, yet quiet. There are three coves that are easy to walk to from the property. Mullion harbour is a delightful example of a Cornish fishing community.	

Trevarrow	
Accommodation	up to 6 people
Family	children/babies OK
Parking	no
Distance to the sea	Less than 100 yards
Reviews: This is a great property with a lot of original features, fantastic view, plus all mod cons. Trevarrow has stood above the beach looking out across the sheltered bay since the 1700's. Roadside parking can be found nearby or in the headland car park.	

TEST 4

Questions 7-14

Complete the summary below.

*Choose **NO MORE THAN THREE WORDS AND/OR A NUMBER** from the passage for each answer.*

Write your answers in boxes 7-14 on your answer sheet.

Glen Cottage

Despite only accommodating **7** _____ you also have use of a **8** _____ where you can sit in a private summerhouse and enjoy looking at the ponds, shrubs, and plants.

Tregonning

You really need to go for more than **9** _____ as there is so much to do here. You don't really need to take anything with you as everything is **10** _____ . If you like **11** _____ then this is the best place to be.

Trevarrow

Of the three cottages it is the closest to **12** _____ and is the only place where you can take **13** _____ but there is no **14** _____ .

SECTION 2   Questions 15-27

Read the text below and answer Questions 15–20.

The London to Brighton Veteran Car Run

The Bonhams London to Brighton Veteran Car Run starts in Hyde Park, London on the first Sunday in November every year. The cars congregate from 6.00am with the first car departing at sunrise (6.56am) and the last car leaving from between 8.00am - 8.30am.

Hyde Park is located in central London and is easily accessible. Cars not associated with the Run and without valid identification will NOT be allowed access to the Park from 5.00am - 12.00pm. Should you wish to show your support at Hyde Park, please enter the park on foot.

How to get to Hyde Park

If you are using a mobile device, the postcode for the park is W2 2UH. This is for guidance only as the park covers a large area.

By Tube
The tube stations that surround Hyde Park are:
- Lancaster Gate (Central Line)
- Marble Arch (Central Line)
- Hyde Park Corner (Piccadilly Line)
- Knightsbridge (Piccadilly Line)

The closest tube station to the VCR start line is Hyde Park Corner.

By Bus
The buses that stop at Hyde Park are:
- North London: 6, 7, 10, 16, 52, 73, 82, 390, 414
- South London: 2, 36, 137, 436
- West London: 9, 10, 14, 19, 22, 52, 74, 148, 414
- East London: 8, 15, 30, 38, 274

By Car
Should you wish to travel by car, there are many car parks located nearby to Hyde Park. The closest car park is situated to the south of Hyde Park and is managed by Q Park. Please contact them directly for prices and location.

The open top bus tours give spectators the opportunity to be involved and experience the 60 mile route taken by the veteran cars. You will be able to soak up the atmosphere at the start line with exclusive access to the paddock area and then follow the cars down the whole route.

Due to the unpredictable British weather the buses will only be filled to 50 per cent capacity giving everyone the opportunity to shelter on the lower deck in the case of inclement weather.

Questions 15-20

Do the following statements agree with the information given in the reading passage?

In boxes 15-20 on your answer sheet, write

TRUE *if the statement agrees with the information*
FALSE *if the statement contradicts the information*
NOT GIVEN *if there is no information on this*

15 The first cars arrive when it is still dark.

16 If you arrive by car to watch the race you can park in Hyde Park.

17 The postcode will take you to the exact place in Hyde Park.

18 If travelling by tube then the Central Line gets you closest to the VCR start line.

19 Tea and light refreshments will be provided on the open top bus.

20 Travelling on the open top bus means you will get wet if it rains.

Read the text below and answer Questions 21-27.

Animal Courtship

Peacock Spiders
Rather like a 6-pack for men, the male peacock spider tries to impress with decorative, colorful abdominal flaps. The spider begins his courtship by vibrating his peacock-like flaps that reveal a pair of black and white third legs. For female peacock spiders nothing could be sexier but males beware because if their courtship goes too far the female, rather like the black widow spider, might eat its mate.

Bowerbirds
Male bowerbirds have to be the ultimate home designers of the animal kingdom. To start their courtship they build an elaborate home called a 'bower'. To make their nest as attractive as possible, bowers have been known to use flowers, berries, seashells, plastic beads, coins, broken glass and even rifle shells. The potential mate can be quite fussy and if not impressed the male will keep adding to his elaborate home to make it more and more colourful.

Northern Cardinals
The male Northern Cardinal will bring bits of food, usually fish, to the bird they are courting and with a tilt of his head, place a tasty snack into her beak. As if this wasn't enough, Cardinals will also take part in what is known as counter singing. Each bird, still within its own territory, will sing to each other by matching and repeating phrases together.

Chameleons
A male chameleon will try to attract a mate by bobbing his head up and down and from side to side to try and get the attention of a potential mate. For males not so sensitive to their progress, the female will show dull colours if she likes him but if not other colours will be shown and he had better run!

Frigates
In addition to waving their heads, flapping their wings and calling to females, the males congregate in large numbers and display their vibrant red throat sacs. For about 20 minutes they force air into these throat sacs, which then resemble a large red balloon. If a male has wooed a female, she will simply fly in and land alongside her new mate.

Hooded seals
Female hooded seals are attracted by males that have the most attractive nasal balloons. Male hooded seals have evolved specialized pinkish-red nasal cavities that they can blow up like bubblegum. To get a female's attention, the male blows up his balloon and starts bouncing it around. The cavities can expand to roughly the size of the seal's head.

Questions 21-27

Look at the following statements and the list of animals below.

Match each statement with the correct animal, *A-F*.

Write the correct letter, *A-F*, in boxes 21-27 on your answer sheet.

NB You may use any letter more than once.

21 This male tries to attract a partner by giving her food.
22 This male likes to look for a partner at the same time as many others.
23 This male might end up being eaten if he's not careful.
24 This male knows if he has been successful or not by the colour of the female.
25 This male likes to do party tricks with his nose.
26 This male likes to think he is a macho man.
27 This male would be a great painter and decorator if he were a man.

	Animals
A	Peacock Spiders
B	Bowerbirds
C	Northern Cardinals
D	Chameleons
E	Frigates
F	Hooded Seals

SECTION 3   Questions 28-40

Read the text below and answer questions 28-40.

The Life of an Amah

Life in China at the beginning of the 20th Century was a very different world than today especially for women. It was often a very hard life with most women working in the rural areas of China for nothing more than a hand-to-mouth living. For many women in Guangdong province by the Pearl River Delta, however, life was to change forever.

The villages they lived in by the Delta that had once been surrounded by fishponds were now replaced by mulberry trees. This meant large quantities of white mulberry leaves to feed silkworms. This was a chance for many women in the area to grab their independence and they did this by working in China's now booming silk industry.

It is estimated that over two million women were involved in the silk industry. They took great pride in their independence and refused a conventional lifestyle. They formed sisterhoods and refused to get married, swore oaths of chastity and moved out of their family homes into spinster houses or vegetarian halls as they were called. Some women even held funeral services for a 'sister' who had decided to marry.

By the 1930s, however, it was all over. The silk industry had been badly affected by the world depression and many of the once thriving factories were forced to close leaving many women jobless. Some managed to maintain their independence by becoming domestic servants. These were the amahs. By moving to Hong Kong, Singapore and other Southeast Asian countries they could earn enough money (5$ a month) to live a reasonable life and continue their independent lifestyle.

An amahs social life took place in a 'coolie fong'. This was a 2-3 story building rented by a sisterhood. It was here where she would spend time after her working day was over or on days off. It was a place to relax, share stories with other 'sisters', hear about new job opportunities, and collect any letters that had been sent to her from her family in China.

Sisterhoods usually ranged in size from six to ten women but could have up to thirty members. The sisterhood networks helped women migrate from the silk areas of China into cities overseas. Once the 'sisters' had arrived in one of these cities, the sisterhoods trained the women in various skills to be a cook, lady's maid or baby amah, and assisted them in finding jobs and in relocating them if their work situation was unsatisfactory. The training provided by the sisterhood usually helped the 'sister' become a valued servant and, therefore, to receive the wages she asked for.

In many ways the sisterhood was similar to a primitive labor union in that members established job definitions and minimum wages for each job. If a member was treated badly by an employer, other 'sisters' refused to work for the employer. Sometimes one sisterhood dominated the domestic staff of a whole apartment building. In such cases the sisterhood controlled who was hired, and if an employer fired a 'sister' without just cause, the sisterhood made it very difficult for the employer to hire another servant.

Sisterhoods also established loan associations for their members, which were especially important for the immigrants separated from possible family assistance. The loan associations also acted as investment clubs where the women pooled their savings to buy property where they could retire together.

Every amah had a different routine as this partly depended on the size of the family they were working for and whether they were European or local. Europeans tended to be more demanding. Some households would hire more than one amah but others would only hire one. For many amahs this was a good thing. Although they had to work harder they felt they were more independent and free of typical domestic servant arguments. These amahs were usually known as "one-leg kick" (or "yat keok tek" in Cantonese) since they did all the work in the household.

A typical workday began when she woke up early in the morning around 5 a.m. and, after getting herself ready, she would start cooking breakfast. After doing the dishes, she swept and tidied up the house. When that was done, she washed the clothes and prepared lunch. After cleaning up, she did the ironing. When that was done, she took a bath. It would then be time to cook again. By the time dinner was over, and she had cleaned up and finished the dishes, it would be about 9p.m. A 16-hour day that was repeated seven days a week with only an occasional half-day off.

Sometimes known as 'black and whites' because they often wore white shirts and black pants with their hair in a bun or a long braid falling down their back, they were seen as an elite group of servants that were hardworking, trustworthy, and completely loyal to the families they worked for.

Stories of their complete loyalty are common with one amah jumping into the sea to rescue her English charge who had accidentally fallen from the ship. Others even worked for free if their employees lost their job and couldn't pay them. In return the amahs were not exploited but treated like members of the family. Indeed, it was their loyalty that led to them being called amah as the Cantonese word for mother is amah.

Questions 28-32

Complete the flow chart below.

Choose **NO MORE THAN THREE WORDS AND/OR A NUMBER** for each answer.

Write your answers in boxes 28-32 on your answer sheet.

Sisterhoods

Sisterhoods usually had up to **28** _____ members

Their networks stretched all the way to **29** _____

Sisterhoods offered training in **30** _____ and help in finding jobs

A trained amah was able to get the **31** _____ she wanted

Sisterhoods acted rather like a **32** _____ controlling salaries

Questions 33-35

Answer the questions below.

Choose **NO MORE THAN TWO WORDS** from the passage for each answer.

Write your answers in boxes 33-35 on your answer sheet.

33 What were silkworms given to eat?
34 Why did many silk factories close?
35 How would sisterhoods help women buy property?

TEST 4

Questions 36-40

Do the following statements agree with the information given in the reading passage?

In boxes 36-40 on your answer sheet, write

> **TRUE** *if the statement agrees with the information*
> **FALSE** *if the statement contradicts the information*
> **NOT GIVEN** *if there is no information on this*

36 Most Amahs never wanted to marry.

37 Amahs would often get letters from China.

38 Some Amahs were called "one-leg kick" because they were kicked by their owners.

39 Amahs were given a regular day off.

40 Amahs were considered the best of the best.

SECTION 1   Questions 1-14

Read the text below and answer Questions 1–7

Ötzi the Iceman

Found in 1991 in the Ötztal Alps this well preserved mummy of a man has been affectionately nicknamed Ötzi the Iceman. He is Europe's oldest natural human mummy and has been estimated to have lived around 3,300 BC.

When first found people thought this was the body of a recently deceased climber. It was only when Ötzi was taken to the University of Innsbruck that it was fairly quickly determined that this was an ancient mummy.

It was finally determined that Ötzi was about 45 years old when he died, weighed 50kg, and was 1.65 metres tall. It was even possible to tell which village he had lived in by the type of pollen and dust grains found on his body.

His diet from several months before he died was determined by hair analysis and shown to be a mixture of different meats, wheat bread, root vegetables, fruits, and other grains. Ötzi's death most likely happened in the spring because of the presence of very fresh pollen that is only seen at this time of year.

High levels of copper and arsenic were also found in his hair suggesting that he might have been involved in making bronze (a mixture of copper, arsenic and/or tin). The copper axe found by his side was probably made by him.

Lines on one of the two fingernails found indicate that he had been ill three times in the last six months.

Ötzi had several tattoos on his body including a cross behind his right knee and various marks around both ankles. These might have been for decoration but it is thought that they are connected to pain relief treatments similar to acupuncture and acupressure.

He wore a cloak made of woven grass and a coat, a belt, a pair of leggings, a loincloth, and shoes, all made of leather of different skins. This was seen as very sophisticated for the time and suggests that Ötzi was a chief of his tribe. The shoes were waterproof and designed for walking across the snow. They were constructed using bearskin for the soles, deer hide for the top panels, and a netting made of tree bark.

TEST 5

Questions 1-7

Complete the summary below.

Choose NO MORE THAN TWO WORDS AND/OR A NUMBER *from the passage for each answer.*

Write your answers in boxes 1-7 on your answer sheet.

Originally thought to be a climber that had **1** _____ not long ago, Ötzi was then found to be an ancient mummy that had lived over 5,000 years ago. Scientists determined the location he had lived in because his body had a certain type of **2** _____ on it. Through **3** _____ we now know that he regularly ate a mixture of different foods including wheat bread and root vegetables. The season he died in was also worked out by the presence of **4** _____ . Ötzi was not in the best of health and had in fact been ill **5** _____ not so long ago as shown by marks on his nails. Different tattoos on his body might have been used for **6** _____ . He was a well dressed man with the type of clothes that suggested he was a tribal **7** _____ .

Read the text below and answer Questions 8-14.

Charles Macintosh

It is difficult to imagine in today's world of high technology but in the 19th century it was impossible to find a waterproof coat. Whenever it rained you were sure to get wet from head to toe. This was all to change with a little help from Charles Macintosh a Scottish chemist and inventor.

Born in 1766, he was expected to spend his life working for his father in the family business dyeing wool and silk. Charles had other ideas, after leaving school, he studied chemistry at a university in Glasgow and after graduating was employed as a clerk with a merchant.

This was only a stepping-stone as Charles never gave up his love of science, particularly chemistry, and spent all of his free time studying. By the time he was twenty Charles had given up his job and had opened up his own company manufacturing various chemicals including ammonium chloride and Prussian blue dye.

This became a successful business for Charles but he was not the kind of man just to focus on one thing. He was constantly looking for better ways, and easier ways to do things and with the help of **James Beaumont Nelson he developed a process to make high quality cast iron. This was an** essential part of the industrial revolution that was happening in Britain at the time and was used to make machines, tools, bridges and ships.

After the death of his father, Charles inherited the family business and began to look for ways to invest his money. Around the same time, in 1817, the Glasgow Gas Light Company was established and Charles became interested in finding a use for the waste products from the coal gas industry. One of these was the waste product known as coal tar naptha. With a touch of genius that perhaps no one else at the time could have thought of Charles combined his knowledge of dyeing material with his love of chemistry.

The result was a liquid rubber that when combined with other textiles made them waterproof. The rainproof cloth was quickly adopted by the British army and navy. It was sold to the public as the world's first raincoat – the Mackintosh. Note the added 'k' to Charles's name.

TEST 5

Questions 8-14

Complete the sentences below.

Choose NO MORE THAN THREE WORDS AND/OR A NUMBER *from the passage for each answer.*

Write your answers in boxes 8-14 on your answer sheet.

8   .... was impossible to buy more than 200 years ago.

9   Macintosh went to university instead of working for the ....

10   By the time he was .... he had started his own company.

11   Macintosh played a big part in the .... that was happening at the time.

12   Coal tar naptha was a .... from the coal gas industry.

13   After some research Macintosh was able to make .... waterproof.

14   The raincoat was finally ready when he added a ....

SECTION 2   Questions 15–27

Read the text below and answer Questions 15–20.

The Treehouse

About the Treehouse

The Treehouse is built from Canadian cedar, Scandinavian redwood and English and Scots pine. It sits high in the treetops among a group of mature lime trees and looks as if it's been there forever.

There are walkways in the sky and wobbly rope bridges, all accessible by wheelchair and buggy. At the heart of the Treehouse is one of the most beautiful and unique restaurants to be found anywhere in the world. There's a roaring log fire in the center of the room, trees growing through the floor, and handcrafted furniture.

About the Treehouse Restaurant

Always featuring local fish and seafood, meats from Northumberland's farmlands and other regional specialities, the Treehouse Restaurant menu highlights local quality, taste and changes throughout the seasons. There's a great wine list, a good range of beers and regular live music.

For a family dining experience that you'll all enjoy, a great night out with friends or a romantic dinner for two, there's nowhere quite like it. We always recommend booking ahead for lunch or dinner.

About the Potting Shed

If you fancy a satisfying lunch, but don't want a full restaurant meal, the Potting Shed is perfect for you. During the day you can grab a drink with some friends, a range of hot and cold delicious light lunch choices, and relax - and all as you take in the unique atmosphere. Choose from classics such as a bacon sandwich, chef's soup of the day, or perhaps some irresistible sweet potato fries.

For a fantastic family lunch, why not eat outside on our Treehouse decking? Just order inside, eat outside - simple as that! Adults can relax to sunshine and birdsong, while kids can dash across rope bridges, run around and enjoy the enchanting walkways.

In the evening the Potting Shed really comes to life, and is open exclusively for our dinner guests to enjoy a pre-dinner drink before moving on to the Restaurant for their meal, or a leisurely nightcap to end the evening.

TEST 5

Questions 15-20

Look at the following statements and the different sections of the Treehouse below.

Match each statement with the correct section, **A-C**.

Write the correct letter, **A-C**, in boxes 15-20 on your answer sheet.

NB You may use any letter more than once.

15 Highlights the lunch time menu
16 It's much better to make a reservation before you go
17 Discusses certain environmentally aspects of the building
18 Their menu focuses on local food
19 Disabled people have easy access
20 This is a great place for children to play

The Treehouse
A About the Treehouse
B About the Restaurant
C About the Potting Shed

Read the text below and answer Questions 21–27.

English Gardens

The English landscape garden is a style of landscape garden which emerged in **England** in the early 18th century, and spread across **Europe** as the principal gardening style of Europe. The English garden was seen as a way to present an idealized view of nature and was influenced by gardens from the East and West.

The National Arboretum
Westonbirt really comes into its own when the trees show off their autumn colour. There are over 16,000 trees and 17 miles of paths at Westonbirt, which also looks its best in spring with displays of rhododendrons, azaleas and magnolias.

Hidcote Manor
This is an Arts & Crafts masterpiece hidden down a series of twisting country lanes in the Cotswolds. It was designed and developed by current owner Maj. Lawrence Johnston, a wealthy, well educated and eccentric American who fought with the British Army in the Boer and First World Wars. Johnston sponsored and participated in plant hunting expeditions around the world to secure rare and exotic species for this extremely pretty garden.

Stourhead
Found in Wiltshire, this is an outstanding example of an 18th century English landscaped garden – not so much rows of flower beds and herbaceous borders, as sweeping lawns, a picturesque lake and temples and a grotto. One of the temples was the location of a rain-soaked (and unsuccessful!) marriage proposal scene in the 2005 film Pride and Prejudice.

Hampton Court Palace
Visitors can get lost in the gardens surrounding Henry VIII's famous palace – literally. There is a maze dating back to about 1700, commissioned by William III. Originally planted using hornbeam trees and later replanted using yew trees, the Hampton Court maze covers a third of an acre, is trapezoid in shape and is the UK's oldest surviving hedge maze.

Sissinghurst Castle Gardens
Visited by Queen Elizabeth in the 16th century, this is one of the most celebrated gardens in the world. Set in the ruins of an Elizabethan house, it offers spectacular views on all sides across the fields and meadows of the Kentish landscape. Close by is the aromatic garden built around a slender brick-built castle tower.

Questions 21-27

Do the following statements agree with the information given in the reading passage?

In boxes 21-27 on your answer sheet, write

TRUE *if the statement agrees with the information*
FALSE *if the statement contradicts the information*
NOT GIVEN *if there is no information on this*

21 The English landscaped garden started in England in the 1800s.

22 Westonbirt is really worth seeing in at least two different seasons.

23 It might be difficult to find Hidcote Manor.

24 The owner of Hidcote manor is quite young.

25 The gardens in Stourhead were first established to film Pride and Prejudice.

26 Henry VIII used to spend a lot of time at Hampton Court Palace.

27 The Elizabethan house in Sissinghurst Castle Gardens has now been rebuilt.

SECTION 3   Questions 28-40

Read the text below and answer Questions 28 – 40.

Coffee

It is not really known when the very first cup of coffee was drunk but there are written records from the 10th century that mention two Arabian philosophers who drank a dark, bitter beverage. At the time it was called bunchum.

Before that it seems that the effects of coffee were well known to warriors in Ethiopa as far back as the 6th century. They would grind the coffee beans into a powder and then mix it with ghee, a kind of clarified butter, and eat it before going into battle. It is generally thought that coffee originates from the forested highlands of Ethiopa and then spread to North Africa, Arabia, and Turkey.

The favorite bedtime story about the origin of coffee goes like this: Once upon a time in the land of Arabia there lived a goat herder named Kaldi. One night, Kaldi's goats failed to come home, and in the morning he found them dancing with abandoned glee near a shiny, dark-leafed shrub with red berries. Kaldi soon determined that it was the red berries that caused the goats' eccentric behavior, and soon he was dancing too.
Finally, a learned imam saw the goats dancing, Kaldi dancing, and the shiny, dark-leafed shrub with the red berries. The learned imam subjected the red berries to various experiments, one of which involved boiling them in water. Soon, neither the imam nor his fellows fell asleep at prayers, and the use of coffee spread from monastery to monastery, throughout Arabia and from there to the rest of the world.

The coffeehouse culture really took off in these areas in the 16th century and became so important that in Turkey not giving your wife enough coffee to drink was seen as a good reason for divorce. Around this time coffee began to spread around the world but to maintain a monopoly all exported coffee beans had to be boiled or partially roasted to prevent other counties from growing them.

However, in the 17th century an Indian pilgrim – a Sufi – called Baba Budan managed to smuggle a few coffee beans out of Arabia and into India. He then established a coffee plantation in the Mysore region of India that still exists today. As of 2009, India produced only 4.5% of the world's coffee but this translates into 8,200 tons of coffee beans per year and an industry that supports more than 250,000 coffee growers.

Although the first coffee house opened in Venice in 1683, coffee had been available since 1608 but was seen as a luxury by all but the very rich. Coffeehouses quickly established a reputation as the place to be seen and a popular meeting place for political debate. The French revolutionists discussed the fate of the bourgeoisie in coffeehouses and if it were not for coffee the founding fathers of the United States of America may never have formed their national policies as they too met in coffeehouses.

In seventeenth-century England, coffeehouses were often called penny universities where, for the price of three pennies (entry and a cup of coffee), you could mix with famous scholars and participate in lively discussions. Later, in the eighteenth and nineteenth centuries, European and American intellectuals spent more time in coffeehouses than they did at home.

When you compare a typical 16th century breakfast in England of beer and herring with coffee, eggs and bread in the 19th century one might be forgiven for thinking that it must have been coffee that fuelled the start of the industrial revolution.

The coffee bean is in fact a seed and comes from a small red (sometimes yellow) fruit that grows on plants halfway in size between a shrub and a tree. The fruit most commonly contains two stones with their flat sides together. A small percentage, about 10%-15% contain a single seed, and this is called a peaberry. Many people believe that they have more flavor than the more common two stone variety.

The two most economically important varieties of coffee plant in the world are the **Arabica** and the **Robusta**; 75-80% of the coffee produced worldwide is Arabica and 20% is Robusta. Arabica seeds consist of 0.8-1.4% **caffeine** and Robusta seeds consist of 1.7-4% caffeine. As **coffee** is one of the world's most widely consumed beverages, coffee seeds are a major **cash crop**, and an important **export** product, counting for over 50% of some developing nations' foreign exchange earnings. The United States imports more coffee than any other nation. The average per capita consumption of coffee in the United States in 2011 was 4.24 kg and the value of coffee imported exceeded $8 billion.

The process that turns these seeds into a beverage is a long and complex process, perhaps the most complex process associated with any major beverage. It starts with the coffee grower, moves to the picker, then to the mill workers who remove the fruit and dry the seeds, then to those who clean and grade the beans, to those who roast them, to the consumers and baristas who finally grind the beans and prepare the beverage.

Every act along the way affects the final taste. Each part of the process can be performed either with passion or with carelessness. The final cup of coffee can, therefore, end up tasting like ditch water or be like nectar that raises your senses to an almost spiritual level of awareness.

Questions 28-31

*Choose the correct letter, **A**, **B**, **C** or **D**.*

Write the correct letter in boxes 28-31 on your answer sheet.

28 How did Arabia maintain their monopoly of coffee?

    A They never exported the beans
    B They boiled the beans
    C They only sold coffee powder
    D They roasted the beans

29 Why was coffee slow to spread through Europe when first introduced?

    A It was seen as an expensive luxury
    B Political reasons
    C There were no coffeehouses
    D It had a bad reputation

30 What were coffeehouses in England also known as?

    A home
    B places for intellectuals
    C cheap places to go
    D penny universities

31 What was a typical breakfast in England in the 16th century?

    A herrings, beer, and coffee
    B beer, bread, and eggs
    C herrings and beer
    D eggs, beer, and herrings

Questions 32-35

Complete the summary below.

*Choose **NO MORE THAN TWO WORDS AND/OR A NUMBER** from the passage for each answer.*

Write your answers in boxes 32-35 on your answer sheet.

Of the two main varieties of coffee plant, more **32** _____ coffee is produced around the world than **33** _____ but the latter has more **34** _____ at **35** _____ .

TEST 5

Questions 36-40

Answer the questions below.

Choose **NO MORE THAN TWO WORDS** from the passage for each answer.

Write your answers in boxes 36-40 on your answer sheet.

36 What did Ethiopian warriors mix coffee powder with before going into battle?
37 According to a famous story, who realised coffee can keep you awake when praying?
38 How many coffee beans did Baba Budan smuggle into India?
39 What type of coffee bean is said to be the most flavourful?
40 If you don't treat coffee properly what can it end up tasting like?

IELTS Reading Answer Sheet

General Reading Test One

You may **photocopy** or **reproduce** this page

		✗	✓			✗	✓
1				21			
2				22			
3				23			
4				24			
5				25			
6				26			
7				27			
8				28			
9				29			
10				30			
11				31			
12				32			
13				33			
14				34			
15				35			
16				36			
17				37			
18				38			
19				39			
20				40			

IELTS Reading Answer Sheet

General Reading Test Two

You may **photocopy** or **reproduce** this page

		✗ ✓			✗ ✓
1			21		
2			22		
3			23		
4			24		
5			25		
6			26		
7			27		
8			28		
9			29		
10			30		
11			31		
12			32		
13			33		
14			34		
15			35		
16			36		
17			37		
18			38		
19			39		
20			40		

IELTS Reading Answer Sheet

General Reading Test Three

You may **photocopy** or **reproduce** this page

#				#			
1				21			
2				22			
3				23			
4				24			
5				25			
6				26			
7				27			
8				28			
9				29			
10				30			
11				31			
12				32			
13				33			
14				34			
15				35			
16				36			
17				37			
18				38			
19				39			
20				40			

IELTS Reading Answer Sheet

General Reading Test Four

You may **photocopy** or **reproduce** this page

		✗ ✓			✗ ✓
1			21		
2			22		
3			23		
4			24		
5			25		
6			26		
7			27		
8			28		
9			29		
10			30		
11			31		
12			32		
13			33		
14			34		
15			35		
16			36		
17			37		
18			38		
19			39		
20			40		

IELTS Reading Answer Sheet

General Reading Test Five

You may **photocopy** or **reproduce** this page

		✗ ✓			✗ ✓
1			21		
2			22		
3			23		
4			24		
5			25		
6			26		
7			27		
8			28		
9			29		
10			30		
11			31		
12			32		
13			33		
14			34		
15			35		
16			36		
17			37		
18			38		
19			39		
20			40		

Answers

Page 9
Nutrition Label
1. tortillas 2. 4% 3. 9 4. less than 2,400mg 5. 220

Page 9 / 10
Index
1. 191 2. 236 3. 132 4. 95 / 116 (**both numbers needed**) 5. 29 6. 67 7. 125 8. 207
9. 124 / 206 (**both numbers needed**)

Pages 13
Expected Answers
1. age 2. something 3. a reason / factor 4. something 5. age 6. something (2x)
7. somebody / name 8. a time

Page 13
Answers
1. 5,500 years old 2. grass 3. stable, cool, dry, (**any two answers followed by** - conditions) 4. sheep dung
5. 600-700 years old 6. leather, grass 7. Ms. Diana Zardaryan 8. 1950s

Page 20
1. vision 2. anomaly 3. project 4. sex 5. democracy 6. research 7. sequence 8. intelligence
9. crises 10. subsided 11. indicates 12. participate 13. ensure 14. assess 15. restore 16. final
17. rational 18. dynamic

Page 21
Method One

Advantages - Differs from person to person.

Disadvantages - You might be working on harder questions and more difficult text first.

Method Two

Advantages - Allows you to select the easier questions first. Adds structure to the text. Makes the harder questions easier by adding structure to the text.

Disadvantages - Differs from person to person.

Pages 26
Answers
1. Mauritius 2. African fruit-eating pigeon 3. tiny wings 4. 100 years 5. museum 6. Naturalists
7. streamline / lithe / active / smart / thin (**any three words**)

Page 28
1. a. proper nouns b. numbers c. italics d. quotations
2. a. title b. subtitle c. chapter/unit headings d. read first sentence
3. a. any word in the heading b. words that appear too many times in the question sentences
4. a. proper nouns b. numbers c. italics d. quotations
5. a. the questions with the best keywords b. questions with obvious answers (proper nouns / numbers)

Page 30
1. 25% / 25 per cent 2. 2,150 trillion kilojoules

Pages 32
1. South-East Asian fishermen / Indonesian fishermen / ancestral aborigines (**any one answer**) 2. drinking water
3. gait / ears / bark (**all three words needed**) 4. food supply 5. Tasmanian tiger / thylacine (**any one answer**)
6. 10 years 7. very young age 8. a pest

Page 33
1. atmosphere 2. electrons and protons

Page 34
1. carbon 2. $700 million

Page 35
1. (just) seven years 2. economic necessity 3. diamond black moth 4. (severe) housing shortages
5. essential 6. Agricultural researchers

Pages 37
1. honour   2. (most) noble weapon   3. kiss   4. fictitious   5. seventy thousand (70,000) horsemen
6. differed considerably   7. 'Seppuku'

Page 38
1. USSR   2. wild boar / wapiti / moose / wolf / brown bears (**any one answer**)   3. Caspian tiger   4. control

Pages 40
1. Saxon period   2. the henge   3. visible today   4. Avebury Trusloe   5. WW2 / World War Two (2)
6. medieval rood-loft   7. manor house   8. archaeological (**need to change the word "archaeology" in the text**)

Page 40
1. regions   2. lighter   3. close   4. protecting (**need to change the word "protect" in the text**)

Page 41
1. large   2. north   3. fighting   4. religious   5. gladiators   6. animal   7. skulls

Pages 42 / 43
1. A - colours   2. B - chymistry   3. B - an embarrassment   4. C - a magician

Pages 44
1. A - they damage their wings   2. D - by using chemicals   3. D - When they walk on chemicals secreted by ants
4. C - exploitative   5. A - start a new colony

Pages 45 / 46
1. B - bread   2. C - encourage civilisation   3. C - Set   4. B - Set   5. D - all of the above

Page 47
1. Correct   2. Correct   3. Wrong   4. Wrong   5. Correct

Page 48
1. postal charges   2. telegraph   3. (mid) 1860s   4. New York   5. (mid) 1870s   6. minutes
7. Bombay

Pages 51
1. 62%   2. 14,684   3. 1,169   4. 28 points higher   5. 43 points higher   6. 37%   7. 26%   8. 35%
9. 39%

Page 52
1. predefined initial combination   2. free text message   3. encrypted message   4. same predefined combination
5. encrypted message   6. upper board

Page 53
1. eye mechanism   2. loose head   3. removed   4. mohair wig   5. eye system
6. chemically cleaned / separated (**any one answer**)   7. old dirt, wax   8. porcelain teeth   9. original eye system
10. cleaned and restyled (**need to change the words "clean" and "restyle" in the text**)   11. period

Page 54
1. 5000 eggs   2. a rudd / a hollow (**any one answer**)   3. die   4. yolk   5. predators   6. salt water
7. five years

Pages 56
1. hear   2. see   3. smell (**1-3 in any order**)   4. Visual   5. Auditory   6. Haptic (**4-6 in any order**)
7. a few seconds   8. short term store   9. response output   10. (about) a minute   11. long term store
12. long periods / many years / minutes to years (**any one answer**)

Pages 59
1. E   2. B   3. D   4. D   5. C   6. A   7. E   8. B   9. F

Pages 61 / 62
1. D   2. F   3. B   4. A   5. C   6. F   7. A   8. B (**this answer is out of order**)   9. D

Page 63
1. C   2. D   3. A   4. B

Page 64
1. TRUE   2. FALSE   3. TRUE   4. NOT GIVEN

Pages 66
1. NOT GIVEN   2. TRUE   3. TRUE   4. FALSE   5. FALSE   6. FALSE   7. NOT GIVEN

Pages 68
1. FALSE   2. NOT GIVEN   3. NOT GIVEN   4. TRUE   5. FALSE   6. TRUE
7. NOT GIVEN   8. TRUE   9. FALSE

Pages 70
1. NO   2. YES   3. NOT GIVEN   4. YES   5. YES

Page 74
1. Crossing the Channel Tunnel   2. Travelling in Style   3. Heaven & Hell

Pages 75
1. i - Bills of Exchange   2. vi - Goldsmith bankers   3. viii - Virginian money   4. iii - Gold standard
5. ix - Intangible money

Page 77
1. ii - Blending therapies   2. x - Splitting colours   3. i - Symbols of emotion   4. vi - Freedom to choose
5. viii - Many positive uses

Page 79
1. 5ml hydrochloric acid   2. cork   3. 50ml graduated cylinder / 50ml glass cylinder   4. 1gm of zinc
5. thistle funnel   6. hydrogen gas   7. test tube   8. tap water

Page 80

1. FILTRATION   2. CRYSTALLIZATION   3. copper oxide powder   4. remove copper oxide / filter copper oxide
5. copper sulphate solution   6. copper sulphate crystals

Five Complete General Reading Tests

TEST ONE - Pages 82 - 94

1. E 2. C 3. A 4. G 5. B 6. D 7. annoying 8. stop talking / talk quietly 9. secrets
10. your distance 11. text messaging 12. queue 13. 350 14. common sense 15. C 16. F
17. B 18. A 19. C 20. E 21. D 22. standards 23. seamless 24. things 25. income
26. praise 27. commitment 28. C 29. B 30. B 31. B 32. press conferences 33. online
34. 3 / three ('additional' does not need to be added to the answer because the word 'further' is used in the summary)
35. 6 / six 36. location 37. food 38. medical procedures 39. communication satellite 40. no return

TEST TWO - Pages 95 - 107

1. southerly 2. art scene 3. London 4. Celtic 5. Lanhydrock 6. tin mine 7. B 8. A
9. D 10. C 11. forewing / forewings 12. antennae 13. hindwing / hindwings 14. pollen basket
15. printing press 16. thousands 17. electronic data 18. hard copy 19. impossible 20. e-book
21. B 22. D 23. A 24. D 25. C 26. E 27. C 28. Joseph Cleaver 29. vocational colleges 30. 2002 31. 2004 32. London 33. 5 institutes 34. video conferencing technology 35. No
36. No 37. Not Given 38. Not Given 39. No 40. Yes

TEST THREE - Pages 108 - 118

1. C 2. B 3. E 4. C 5. A 6. D 7. Not Given 8. False 9. Not Given 10. True
11. False 12. False 13. False 14. True 15. sightseeing 16. queue 17. one pass
18. Travelcard 19. money back guarantee 20. Thames River Cruise 21. £24.00 22. B 23. C
24. C 25. C 26. B 27. A 28. F 29. I 30. B 31. J 32. D 33. ring in the nose
34. friendship 35. to beg 36. a package holiday 37. be flexible / adapt (either answer) 38. educate yourself 39. trash 40. potentially destructive practices

TEST FOUR - Pages 119 - 130

1. correct fee 2. enrolment form 3. call you back 4. one week 5. VAT 6. insufficient enrolments
7. 2 / two 8. beautiful landscaped garden 9. one week 10. provided 11. fishing 12. the sea
13. babies 14. parking 15. True 16. False 17. False 18. False 19. Not Given
20. False 21. C 22. E 23. A 24. D 25. F 26. A 27. B 28. 30 / thirty
29. China 30. various skills 31. wages 32. (primitive) labor union 33. (white) mulberry leaves
34. world depression 35. investment clubs 36. True 37. Not Given 38. False 39. False
40. True

TEST FIVE - Pages 131 - 142

1. recently deceased 2. pollen 3. hair analysis 4. pollen 5. 3 / three times 6. pain relief 7. chief
8. A waterproof coat 9. family business 10. 20 / twenty 11. industrial revolution 12. waste product
13. textiles 14. k 15. C 16. B 17. A 18. B 19. A 20. C 21. False
22. True 23. True 24. False 25. False 26. Not Given 27. False 28. B 29. A 30. D
31. C 32. Arabica 33. Robusta 34. caffeine 35. 1.7 - 4% 36. ghee / clarified butter
37. learned imam 38. a few 39. peaberry 40. ditch water

Acknowledgments - Texts

page 5 – The Wreck
http://www.deepimage.co.uk/

page 8 – Colditz
http://www.historylearningsite.co.uk/

page 10 – Index
http://thepencilpoint.com/

page 12 – The Tea Trade
http://www.tea.co.uk/

pages 14/15 – World's oldest leather shoe found in Armenia
http://www.alphagalileo.org/
Release issued by University College Cork, Ireland

page 17 – San Francisco Earthquake
http://mary-trotter-kion.suite101.com/

page 20 – University Vocabulary Level Checks
Batia Laufer & Paul Nation.
http://www.lextutor.ca/

page 22/23 – 26 – The Dodo
http://www.dodopad.com/

page 30 – US food waste worth more than offshore drilling
http://www.newscientist.com

pages 31/32 – The Dingo – An Australian Pest
http://www.aussie-info.com/

page 33 – The Northern Lights
http://www.northernlightscentre.ca/northernlights.html

page 34 – Sea-otters worth 700million in carbon credits
http://www.newscientist.com/

page 35 – Cuba's Organic Revolution
http://www.ru.org/

pages 36/37 – The Samurai of Japan and European Knights
http://www.bukisa.com/

page 39 – Avebury
http://www.avebury-web.co.uk/

pages 41 – Roman Remains
http://www.yorkarchaeology.co.uk/

page 42 – Sir Isaac Newton and Alchemy
http://www.bukisa.com/

pages 43/44 – Ants secrete aphid tranquilizer from their feet
http://scienceblogs.com/

page 45 – Osiris
http://www.menumagazine.co.uk/

page 48 – Changes in Industrial Britain
http://www.casebook.org/

pages 49/50 – Single sex vs. Coeducational High Schools
http://newsroom.ucla.edu/

page 52 – Enigma Machine
www.2worldwar2.com/

page 53 – Doll Restoration
Doll Doctor, Gary Sowatzka
http://www.sowatzka.com/

pages 55/56 – Memory
http://my.ilstu.edu/

pages 57/58 – The Origin of Language
http://www.chrisknight.co.uk/

pages 60/61 – The Penny Black
Robert Murray Stamp Shop, Edinburgh
www.stamp-shop.com/

page 63 – The Unexplained Powers of Animals
http://www.ru.org/

page 64 – The Saiga Antelope
http://www.newscientist.com/

pages 65/66 – Have Researchers Created Synthetic Life at the J. Craig Venter Institute?
http://www.associatedcontent.com/

pages 67/68 – Alaskans' vitamin D production slows to a halt
Geophysical Institute
http://www.gi.alaska.edu/

page 69/70 – Coral Triangle
http://www.ru.org/

page 72 – Northern Lights
Geophysical Institute
http://www.gi.alaska.edu/

page 72 – Problems with the Asteroid Theory
http://www.articlesbase.com/

page 72 – Tea in China ' Tea in Japan
http://newsroom.ucla.edu/

page 73 – Desertification
http://www.ypte.org.uk/

page 74 – Crossing the Channel Tunnel
http://www.seat61.com/

page 74 – Aboard the Titanic
http://www.titanic-facts.com/

page 74 - Heaven and Hell
Active Travel Asia
http://www.visitangkortemples.com/

page 76 – Money
http://projects.exeter.ac.uk/

page 78 – Colour through the Ages
http://www.colourtherapyhealing.com/

Acknowledgments - Images

All images - unless otherwise stated - were provided by Wikimedia Commons and are, therefore, under free license or in the public domain.

page 4
http://danidraws.com/

page 14

page 17

page 22

page 35

page 36

page 44

page 56
http://my.ilstu.edu/

page 57

page 60

page 76

pages 79/80
http://www.btinternet.com/~chemistry.diagrams/gas_preparations.htm

General Reading Tests
Acknowledgments - Texts

TEST 1
Mobile Phone Etiquette
http://www.wikihow.com/Practice-Cell-Phone-Etiquette

Savants
http://m.neatorama.com/2008/09/05/10-most-fascinating-savants-in-the-world/#!OS4po

Job Sharing
http://workingmoms.about.com/od/workschedule/a/JobSharing.htm

Mission to Mars
http://www.mars-one.com/mission/roadmap

TEST 2
Cornwall
http://www.visitcornwall.com/essentials#.Uzk12qiSy4E

Bees
http://www.unionsafety.eu/docs/HSNewsItems%2013/BritishBeesUnderThreatFromPesticidesSaysFriendsOfTheEarth.html

The Printing Process
https://www1.lightningsource.com/process.aspx

Yoga
http://www.dailycupofyoga.com/2012/06/09/5-different-types-of-yoga-which-one-suits-you-the-best/

British Study Centres
http://www.british-study.com/adults/english-language-schools/oxford/

TEST 3
Gourmet Restaurants
http://www.reviewcentre.com/products4398.html

GREGGS Bakery
https://www.greggs.co.uk/about-us/faq/#question2

The London Pass
http://www.londonpass.com/?aid=17&gclid=CJHEs6yYub4CFZIrvQod7VsASw

The Body Shop
http://en.wikipedia.org/wiki/The_Body_Shop

Ecotourism
http://untamedpath.com/eco-tours/eco-travel-guidelines.shtml

General Reading Tests
Acknowledgments - Texts

TEST 4
How to Book a Course
http://www.cornwall.gov.uk/education-and-learning/adult-and-community-education/adult-education-courses/?page=2112&altTemplate=_Standard

Holiday Cottages
http://www.cornishcottageholidays.co.uk/html/property_list.php?list_area_id=5&cmd=area

The London to Brighton Veteran Car Race
http://www.veterancarrun.com/event-info

Animal Courtship
http://www.huffingtonpost.com/2014/02/13/weird-animal-courtship-displays_n_4761381.html
http://kidscorner.org/html/zoo0206.php

The Life of an Amah
http://journeytoforever.org/edu_silk_amah.html
http://cwh.ucsc.edu/SocialBio.Chan.pdf

TEST 5
Ötzi the Iceman
http://en.wikipedia.org/wiki/%C3%96tzi

Charles Macintosh
http://iainthepict.blogspot.com/2011/07/charles-macintosh.html

The Treehouse
http://www.alnwickgarden.com/explore/whats-here/the-treehouse/potting-shed

English Gardens
http://www.nationaltrust.org.uk/sissinghurst-castle/

Coffee
http://www.coffeereview.com/reference.cfm?ID=12

www.ingramcontent.com/pod-product-compliance
Lightning Source LLC
Chambersburg PA
CBHW080921180426
43192CB00040B/2607